Nuer Journeys, Nuer Lives

Sudanese Refugees in Minnesota

Second Edition

Jon D. Holtzman
Western Michigan University

PEARSON

Boston • New York • San Francisco
Mexico City • Montreal • Toronto • London • Madrid • Munich • Paris
Hong Kong • Singapore • Tokyo • Cape Town • Sydney

Series Editor: Dave Repetto
Series Editorial Assistant: Jack Cashman
Marketing Manager: Laura Lee Manley
Production Editor: Roberta Sherman
Editorial-Production Services: GGS Book Services
Composition Buyer: Linda Cox
Manufacturing Buyer: Debbi Rossi
Cover Administrator: Elena Sidorova
Electronic Composition: GGS Book Services

For related titles and support materials, visit our online catalog at www.ablongman.com

Between the time Web site information is gathered and then published, it is not unusual for some sites to have closed. Also, the transcription of URLs can result in typographical errors. The publisher would appreciate notification where these errors occur so that they may be corrected in subsequent editions.

Library of Congress Cataloging-in-Publication Data
Holtzman, Jon.
    Nuer journeys, Nuer lives: Sudanese refugees in
Minnesota / by Jon D. Holtzman. — 2nd ed.
        p. cm. — (New immigrants series)
    Includes bibliographical references.
    ISBN-13: 978-0-205-54332-8
    ISBN-10: 0-205-54332-4

1. Sudanese Americans—Minnesota—Social life and customs. 2. Nuer (African people)—Minnesota—Social life and customs. 3. Refugees—Minnesota. 4. Sudan—Emigration and immigration. 5. Minnesota—Emigration and immigration. I. Title.

F615. S77H65 2007
977. 6'004927624—dc22   2007000384

Printed in the United States of America
10 9 8 7 6 5 4   11 10 09

Dedication

To Samuel Holtzman
For his journey, and his life in an unfamiliar land.

Contents

Foreword to the Series

The United States is now in the midst of the largest wave of immigration in the nation's history. Recent immigrants from Asia, Latin America, and the Caribbean are changing the American ethnic landscape.

Since the late 1960s, America has, once again, become a country of large-scale immigration, the vast majority coming from Asia, Mexico, Central and South America, and the Caribbean. The number of foreign-born is at an all-time high: an estimated 35 million immigrants were living in the United States in 2005. Although immigrants are a smaller share of the nation's population than they were at the beginning of the twentieth century—12 percent in 2005 compared to 15 percent in 1910—recent immigrants are having an especially dramatic impact because their geographic concentration is so great. Despite the increasing dispersal of immigrants since the 1990s, six states—California, New York, Florida, Texas, New Jersey, and Illinois—still accounted for two-thirds of the immigrant population in 2005. Los Angeles, New York, Miami, Chicago, San Francisco, Houston, and Washington, D.C. are, increasingly, immigrant cities with new ethnic mixes. And it is not just America's major urban centers that are experiencing immigrant inflows. Many smaller cities and towns also have growing immigrant populations.

Who are the new immigrants? What are their lives like here? How are they redefining themselves and their cultures? And how are they contributing to a new and changing America? The *New Immigrants Series* provides a set of case studies that explores these themes among a variety of groups. The books in the series are written by recognized experts who have done extensive in-depth research on particular immigrant groups. The groups represent a broad range of today's arrivals, coming from a variety of countries and cultures. The studies, based on research done in different parts of the country, cover a wide geographical range, from New York to California.

The books in the series are, first and foremost, ethnographies. All draw on qualitative research that shows what it means to be an immigrant in America today. As part of each study, individual immigrants tell their stories, which helps give a sense of the experiences and problems of the newcomers. Through the case studies, a dynamic picture emerges of the way immigrants are carving out new lives for themselves at the same time as they are creating a new and more diverse America.

Ethnographic case studies provide a depth often lacking in research on immigrants in the United States. Moreover, many of the authors in the *New Immigrants Series* have done research in the country of origin as well as in the United States. Having field experience at both ends of the migration chain makes ethnographers particularly sensitive to the role of transnational ties that link immigrants to their home societies. Firsthand experience of immigrants in their home cultures also enables ethnographers to appreciate continuities as well as changes in the immigrant setting.

Given immigrants' important and ever-growing presence in American society, it becomes more crucial than ever to learn about their experiences and to hear their voices. The case studies in the *New Immigrants Series* will help readers understand the cultures and lives of the newest Americans and bring out the complex ways that recent immigrants are coming to terms with and creatively adapting to life in a new land.

NANCY FONER
Series Editor

Acknowledgments

There are many people and institutions who have played an important role in making this book possible. The research on which this book was based was generously funded by a Postdoctoral Fellowship of the International Migration Program of the Social Science Research Council, with funds provided by the Andrew Mellon Foundation. Additional funding for the research was provided through a research grant from the Minnesota Historical Society.

I would like to thank the many Nuer who have inspired this work, and who have made it possible by letting me into their homes and their lives. I would like to give particular thanks to Dobuol Deng, whose friendship and formal assistance throughout the project were integral to its success. I would also like to thank the many Minnesotans from churches, social services, and the local community who have helped me in this project, and who have generously shared their experiences in working with the Nuer.

Nancy Foner has been integral to the completion of this book, from her first suggestion that I write it through her careful and thoughtful editing. Douglas Johnson's help with photographic sources is greatly appreciated, as is the help of Wal and Julia Duany. Sharon Hutchinson's comments on a related manuscript were extremely useful in putting into focus contemporary Nuer life in Sudan, and the changes which have occurred in Minnesota. Various colleagues, particularly Sarah Hill, have made very useful suggestions for changes and additions to this new edition. This book also would not have been possible without the diffuse support of Bilinda Straight, not to mention her careful and repeated reading of the manuscript. Without the friendship and hospitality afforded me by the Samburu during research in Kenya, I might never have been so eager to make contact with the Nuer community in Minnesota, and they deserve repeated thanks. I wish to thank my parents, Jordan and Joyce Holtzman, for everything they have done for me. Finally, there is the joy which Clare Rose Straight Holtzman has provided in devoting much of her first three years to her father's anthropological research.

Preface:
Commuting to Nuerland

"Smell," wrote Rousseau, "is the sense of memory and desire." Similarly, twentieth century psychologists and other students of perception have noted the unique power of smell to evoke and essentialize experience. Uniquely among the human senses, smell has the capacity to capture a time and place in a way that our other senses do not. Smell can be a rich, multi-layered symbol, a vehicle which can transport you to real and idealized places, distant in time and space. Linked in complex ways to memory and emotion in the human mind, the smell of a school lunch pizza can make you feel you are ten again; the stale smell of post-party beer and wine can return you to college; the pungent manure of the family farm can bring you home. For anthropologists, the intensity of fieldwork can also crystallize the character- istic smells of their research sites. Thus, for instance, a smell that I take to be "Samburu" was burned indelibly into my memory over the course of my research in their herding com- munities in northern Kenya: a rich but sweet mixture of milk, leather, sweat, and smoke. On the road back to the Samburu District I have often smelled the settlements before I even saw them, and could be happy in being back. And even now, being far away, a sniff of a Samburu calabash, or the leather handle of my Samburu knife, has the capacity to transport me back again.

There is, too, a smell that in my mind is Nuer, a smell I encountered in approaching virtually every Nuer home, and instantly evokes remembrances of the Nuer. Perhaps in Sudan—the ancestral home of the Nuer, where anthropologists have immortalized them as cattle-keeping people—the smell I would take to be Nuer might be much like the Samburu smell I know so well, one of leather, milk, and dung fires. Yet instead the smell that instantly transports me to "fieldwork among the Nuer" is a very different one, a combination of paint, cleaning agents, carpet, and the wide array of different foods cooked in kitchens in close proximity to one another. In point of fact, the smell is not distinctively Nuer, but is common to many lower income, suburban apartments, particularly of a 1970s vintage, which are the current homes of Nuer who have resettled as refugees in Minnesota.

Smells are not, of course, my main concern in this book. But as anthropologist Paul Stoller (1997) has argued, the sensuous aspects of field sites—the sounds, tastes, smells, and the like—convey not only the experience of fieldwork, but also, more importantly, vividly capture and represent the nature of the places anthropologists study. Here, I suggest, they provide a particularly useful way to appreciate the radically changing nature of both the subject matter and practice of anthropology, in the context of globalization and international migration. The smell I have internalized in my Kenyan research as Samburu is a smell consonant with the traditional subject of anthropology; that is, a relatively remote rural community, characterized by a distinctive way of life based in unique practices and beliefs. In contrast, the smell I have internalized as Nuer has little to do with the distinctive cultural patterns of the people who have long been perhaps the most famous case study in Africanist anthropology, if not in anthropology as a whole. Rather, the smell I associate with the Nuer is a product of the class position they now occupy in the American society they have newly joined.

Especially since the 1990s anthropologists have paid particular attention to the implications of the increasingly rapid movement of people and ideas around the globe for the practice of anthropology. Akhil Gupta and James Ferguson (1997) have noted how such developments have disrupted the association anthropologists typically assumed of cultures, peoples and places, such that Indians (and hence Indian culture) was inexorably in and of India, Chinese in and of China, and so forth. Certainly this longstanding assumption was overstated even of the past, given the historical importance of diasporic populations and global cultural flows (Mintz 1997). However, the exponential intensification of such development in recent decades means that more and more this seemingly natural conjunction of people, places, and cultures is disrupted, with individuals and groups increasingly constituted through multiple layers of identity, their communities spread across cities, countries, and the globe. Thus, where it was once possible to study the Nuer in their home area without much reference to the Nuer who lived elsewhere, today this is impossible. If previously, the tree in western Nuerland beneath which the Nuer said that humanity emerged was a salient spatial marker of Nuer identity, American cities for refugee resettlement—such as the Twin Cities or more recently Omaha—have become key geographical sites of Nuer culture for Nuer in dispersed locales throughout the United States. As Gupta and Ferguson (among others) also emphasize, this dispersal of populations has important implications for the practice of anthropological research. It means that anthropologists find they cannot answer many central questions by simply sitting in the center of a rural village selected for long-term fieldwork, talking to their neighbors and watching the daily routines and occasional dramas unfold. Going to the field may, instead, involve getting on a subway, commuting between dispersed families in American suburbs, or following transnational migrants on their treks.

These same developments have posed challenges for anthropological analysis, which I have tried to engage with in this book. Anthropology is a discipline that has long gained much of its power from its attention to the exotic, or to use a slightly less charged phrase, attention to difference. Anthropology has developed with a central goal of understanding human cultural diversity as part of its quest to understand fundamentally what it means to be human, but also to show that however natural our own practices and beliefs seem to us, they represent only one tiny point in the vast constellation of cultural forms existing throughout the globe. In fact, cultural anthropology's greatest popularizer, Margaret Mead, is best known for her study of Samoan adolescence, which was explicitly written to show that the assumption that the turbulent teenage years are a "natural" part of growing up is wrong. Mead (1928) argued, instead, that the turbulence of the teen years in the United States was a product of our culture, and not found among Samoans, mainly because they were less concerned about regulating the sexuality of adolescents. Today, anthropology's key goal of exploring different and contrasting versions of human experience is seen as being threatened by globalization, which, it is feared, will lead to increasing sameness and homogenization of culture. Bob Dylan once asserted that, since he wasn't different from anyone else, "There ain't no use in talkin' to me, you might as well be talkin' to you." One might similarly ask that if the Nuer in Minnesota are dealing with issues of cars, child care costs, and the like—just like many other Americans—what do we gain by studying them as Nuer?

Micaela di Leonardo (2000) raises similar questions in her discussion of the practice of ethnography in U.S. settings. In "Exotics at Home," she argues that the ethnography of groups in the United States has for decades suffered from a tendency for anthropologists to transport their paradigm of the exotic and culturally unusual to studies at home. They focus on an Other—for instance, immigrants, minorities, and the underclass—who are quite different from most anthropologists, who tend to have white, middle-class backgrounds. In continuing to harbor a concern for the culturally exotic, di Leonardo argues, anthropologists miss and misconstrue central aspects of class and the practice of everyday life which are most critical to analyses of contemporary American society.

Di Leonardo's critique is well worth considering in regard to issues raised in this book and elsewhere, though there are of, course, different perspectives, that stress the continued importance of cultural difference. As global processes undermine certain types of cultural diversity, anthropologists and others have argued that these same global processes can also become sources of new forms of diversity. Thus even a product as emblematic of American cultural hegemony as Coca Cola—indeed, the global spread of American popular culture is sometimes referred to as "Coca Colonization"—can take on new local meanings in cultural contexts around the globe. For instance in Trinidad many believe that Coca Cola is a quintessentially local drink, not even realizing its origins are American at all (Miller 1998). Among Orang Ulu, the native inhabitants of the interior of Borneo, wrestler Hulk Hogan has become a kind of mythological culture hero (Metcalf 2001). Ted Swedenburg and Smadar Lavie (1996) point to the relevance of these kinds of developments for anthropology today when they ask rhetorically what Margaret Mead would make of Samoan gangs in Los Angeles, and Samoan gangsta rappers going by names such as the Boo Ya Tribe, a term derived from the Samoan onomatopoetic rendering of a shotgun blast at a driveby shooting.

The issues that Swedenburg and Lavie raise have implications for our understanding of the Nuer in the pages that follow. How much of the Nuer lives described here can be explained by their position on the lower rungs of American society and economy? How much to their experiences negotiating international bureaucracies concerned with the care and resettlement of refugees? And how much to their cultural background, to their past life experiences in rural Africa, to being Nuer? Sorting through such issues is in many ways central to the project of cultural anthropology in an age characterized by movement of people and ideas around the globe on a scale unprecedented in human history.

The rapid culture change that often accompanies globalization places the dynamism of contemporary human cultures in stark relief. Anthropologists have until recently often ignored the fact that ethnographies are not just portraits of a people, but portraits of a people at a point in time. Indeed, in anthropology textbooks it still remains commonplace to talk about "the Zuni" or "the Yanamamo" without any mention that these are the Zuni of the 1920s, or the Yanamamo of the 1960s, who might have quite different worldviews and ways of life than those of today, or for that matter those in earlier periods. Hopefully, the contrast between the Nuer in these pages and the well known "traditional" life of the Nuer serves to illustrate the dynamism of contemporary human cultures.

At the same time, it is important not to simply substitute one snapshot of the Nuer for another—and end up, for example, replacing the famous image of the leopard skin chief with one of newly arrived refugees huddled around a Barney video in the frozen north. Just as our most familiar images of the Nuer are products of E.E. Evans-Pritchard's encounters with them in the 1930s, so are the images in this book the product of a particular anthropologist's encounter with particular Nuer in a particular place, and most notably at a particular time—principally the late 1990s, though updated with ongoing developments through the present for this edition. Thus, the dynamism illustrated in this book by the radical changes in what it means to be Nuer from the 1930s to the present remains an ongoing process. At the moment that you read, the Nuer who inhabit these pages are not precisely the same Nuer that inhabit the northern suburbs of the Twin Cities, for, as with everyone, their lives are ever-changing. This is a book, then, not so much about remade lives as it is about remaking lives, not just about journeys that have been taken but also about ones that continue to unfold.

Nuer Journeys, Nuer Lives

Introduction

It is 85 degrees, or as high as the thermostat will go, in the darkened apartment. As the early evening syndicated TV lineup moves from the Mighty Morphin Power Rangers through the Simpsons, Ganwar[1] shows me his hand and describes the circumstances in which his thumb was shot off in the Sudanese civil war. On the carpet nearby, his wife Nyapen—her face intricately decorated with patterns of pinpoint scarification known as *bir*—sits with their six-month-old son, as he plays in front of her. Three older children and a male relative in his early twenty's mill about the house, watching TV, eating peanut butter sandwiches, and preparing the evening meal of rice and fish.

The contrast between this scene and the former realities of Ganwar's life in Africa is striking. Born in a rural village in southern Sudan, there was no school in the area where Ganwar grew up, and he spent his days the way any young Nuer might, playing freely around the village, climbing trees, making clay cows to play with and, as he grew older, gradually acquiring more responsibility for the care of his family's cows, sheep, and goats. Initiated into manhood through the cutting of the six deep scars—*gaar*—which are still prominent on his forehead, Ganwar later married and assumed a position of leadership as one of the village's

---

[1]All names appearing in this book are pseudonyms.

chiefs. But when the civil war came to his area, Ganwar led the villagers to fight alongside the rebels. He was wounded and fled to nearby Ethiopia, beginning the long, strange journey which has brought him and his family to Minnesota. Now, as we sit together discussing his past life, we also discuss the job which he recently lost, his current situation with welfare, and mull over how he will pay this month's rent.

The Nuer, who historically have been one of the most important case studies in anthropology, are now among America's newest immigrant groups. Refugees from the bloody civil war in southern Sudan, the Nuer began to resettle in the United States in the early and mid 1990s. Though few in number, the Nuer present a new and compelling case study of the American immigrant experience. As a population from rural Africa, they stand in contrast to historically important immigrant populations to the United States while, at the same time, they are representative of the growing number of groups from sub-Saharan Africa who are resettling in the United States. This book will explore the experiences of the Nuer as they struggle to find a place, and make sense of life, in an unfamiliar land.

THE NUER

The Nuer have been well known to generations of anthropologists from accounts of their traditional life in southern Sudan (Evans-Pritchard 1940; 1951; 1956). The Nuer are agro-pastoralists from southern Sudan, who subsist on a mixed economy of animal husbandry and cultivation. They are classified as members of the Nilotic cultural/linguistic group, which includes the Luo and Turkana of Kenya, the Karimijong of Uganda, and their neighbors the Dinka, from whom the Nuer are believed to have diverged only in recent centuries (Kelly 1985). Current population figures estimate that there are now over a million Nuer (Hutchinson 1996), and they are the second largest ethnic group in southern Sudan.

The Nuer may well be the most important case study in the history of anthropology. They are best known through the work of E. E. Evans-Pritchard, the first anthropologist to work in Africa using the now well-accepted research methods of long-term fieldwork and participant observation. Based on research beginning in 1930, Evans-Pritchard wrote three ethnographies which are now classics within anthropology—*The Nuer* (1940) which focused principally on political life, *Marriage and Kinship Among the Nuer* (1951), and *Nuer Religion* (1956). The combination of detailed ethnography and incisive theoretical analysis have made these works exceedingly important in their own right. In fact, the Nuer have become a sort of touchstone in anthropology, and scholars have returned to and reanalyzed Evans-Pritchard's Nuer research again and again (e.g., Sahlins 1961; Beidelman 1966, 1971; Gough 1971; Southall 1986; Newcomer 1972; Karp and Maynard 1983; Kelly 1985). Even today, discussions of the Nuer of Evans-Pritchard's time continue to be found in scholarly debates and theoretical writings, in graduate training programs of anthropology departments throughout the world, and in the teaching of anthropology at the introductory level. Indeed, virtually all introductory textbooks in anthropology make reference (and usually multiple references) to the Nuer as a central example for various aspects of human culture.

That several hundred Nuer now live in Minnesota—and many more in other Midwestern cities and elsewhere around the United States—testifies to the dramatic changes which have occurred since Evans-Pritchard's time. Not everything has changed, however, and many aspects of Nuer culture described in the 1930s remain important. The thatched hut villages in which Nyapen and Ganwar grew up in the 1970s amongst their cattle did not differ strikingly from those of Evans-Pritchard's time, and, before the war, life remained centered on the daily routine of cultivation and animal husbandry.

Among the most striking features of Nuer culture discussed in Evans-Pritchard's work is their emphasis on cattle, which remains central to Nuer cultural values. The first substantive chapter of the first book in the trilogy of classics focuses directly on what he terms the Nuer's "interest in cattle." He writes:

> . . . the only labour in which they delight is the care of cattle. They not only depend on cattle for many of life's necessities but have the herdsman's outlook on the world. Cattle are their dearest possession

and they gladly risk their lives to defend their herds
or to pillage those of their neighbours. Most of their
social activities concern cattle, and cherchez la
vache [look at the cows] is the best advice that can
be given to those who desire to understand Nuer
behaviour (1940: 16).

Evans-Pritchard discusses at length the central significance
of cattle in all aspects of Nuer life. Cattle are central to Nuer
economic life, by providing milk, meat, hides, as well as dung
which is used as fuel. Even more importantly, cattle are the central means for defining social relationships. Cattle are owned
principally within a family, but at the same time serve to tie
together a broader network of kin. The tribal and clan divisions
within Nuer political organization are defined largely in terms
of access to pastures and water supplies required for their
herds, and feuds between political subgroupings most frequently revolve around issues of cattle. Youth take "ox names"
to define their own personal identity and sing praise songs
concerning their cattle. Because of their importance within
Nuer culture, the Nuer possess an amazingly rich vocabulary
to distinguish between cattle, with ten color terms, twenty-five
terms to describe the patterns of markings, six basic terms to
describe the shape of horns, and many others to discuss the sex
and age of the animal. Perhaps most importantly, marriages
are enacted through the payment of forty bridewealth cattle
from the family of the groom to the family of the bride. All
social relationships, Evans-Pritchard (1940) argued, were in
some way centrally concerned with the exchange of cattle,
rights in cattle, or factors related to the necessity of cattle husbandry, such that he states: "Their social idiom is a bovine
idiom." A recent ethnographer has described this in another
way, stating that (at the time of Evans-Pritchard's research)
"cattle and people were one" (Hutchinson 1992).

Other striking features of the Nuer and their way of life
have also made them a fascinating case study for generations of anthropologists. Many Nuer are physically impres-
sive, with a tendency to be quite tall and exceptionally long
limbed—a fact that physical anthropologists explain as an
effective means of regulating body heat in their Sahelian
environment. Indeed, his exceptional reach enabled Manute

Bol, of the closely related Dinka ethnic group, to become one of the National Basketball Association's (NBA) leading shot blockers for a number of seasons in the 1980s. In Evans-Pritchard's time the Nuer wore little or no clothing; the Nuer are frequently portrayed nude, with little on their bodies but a few beads and the white ash of dung fires in which they bathe their bodies and that accentuates their striking physiques. The Nuer reputation for warfare—both for cattle raiding and as an expansionist enterprise to capture new pastures—has further served to fix their place in the anthropological imagination. Several famous and influential works in anthropology, in fact, focus on the question of what aspects of Nuer society enable them to be so effective in warfare against culturally similar neighbors possessing identical martial technology (Sahlins 1961; Kelly 1985).

Much has been written about the feature of Nuer social organization that anthropologists have termed the "segmentary lineage." Politically, the Nuer are organized into patrilineal clans and lineages, groups of people who are tied together by real or putative descent from a common male ancestor. These clans and lineages—which anthropologists term descent groups—may have rights as a corporate unit to wells or pastures and be associated with the particular area where they live. These descent groups can be thought of as family trees, which may be divided into many different branches or segments. For instance, your grandfather might be considered the founder of a lineage while all his sons (your father and your uncles) would be founders of sublineages within it. Their sons (your brothers and your male cousins) could be founders of more sublineages. This system is able to fuse large numbers of people into a single cohesive system, so that all Nuer can ostensibly fit within a single genealogy. Within this system alliances and mutual assistance are determined based on the closeness of descent groups. Anthropologists commonly explain this through the dictum "Me against my brother; me and my brother against my cousin; me, my brother, and my cousin against the world." Anthropologists have argued that the segmentary lineage system is a particularly effective means through which stateless societies, such as the traditional Nuer, can organize large numbers of people in warfare and, therefore, helps to explain their expansionist successes.

Traditional Nuer, such as these pictured in the 1920s, continue to be a mainstay of anthropological thought.

While most of our knowledge of the Nuer is based on Evans-Pritchard's classic studies, and subsequent reanalyses of his material by other scholars, recent studies have shed new light on Nuer life. Most important is the work of Sharon Hutchinson, who began her fieldwork among the Nuer in the early 1980s. Hutchinson explores topics which were largely ignored in Evans-Pritchard's work—for instance Nuer gender relations—as well as detailing the many changes in Nuer life since the 1930s. Over the course of fifty years, Nuer culture and society has changed in many ways. Once an independent tribal people, they have been transformed to assume the identity of an ethnic group subsumed within the Sudanese nation state. Other important changes include the introduction of money, western education and Christianity, widespread migratory wage labor of young men going to cities like Khartoum, the expansion of local cattle markets, the spread of government control to formerly remote areas of Nuerland, and, perhaps most striking, the chronic and bloody civil war that erupts regularly between the south and the Muslim/Arab north, which is discussed in the next section.

Some of the most interesting findings in Hutchinson's (1996) study illustrate the ways in which marriage and gender relations have changed over the course of half a century. One factor underlying this has been the introduction of government courts, which have reinterpreted Nuer customs concerning marriage and divorce. Another factor with broad impact has been the introduction of money and its significance as a form of wealth accessible outside of the traditional cattle economy. In the 1930s, "cattle and people were one," inexorably tied together in an intricate web of economic and social relations, in religious formulations, and in symbolic conceptualizations of human identity. By the 1980s, the widespread use of money and the commodification of Nuer cattle had begun to sever this equivalence. In the past, cattle could principally be acquired only through forms of exchange within the local community, such as inheritance and bridewealth payments which served to circulate livestock within the community's network of human relationships. With the creation of cattle markets, the introduction of money, and migratory wage labor of young men, cattle could now be acquired directly through the market economy, and this had enormous implications for relations between men and women, old and young, and, more generally, for Nuer kinship networks. Where once there was a seamless circulation of people and cattle, new rifts and tensions developed as it became possible to circumvent the traditional system.

THE WAR IN SUDAN

The Nuer in the United States are refugees from the bloody and protracted Sudanese civil war. This war has pitted southern Sudanese groups (such as the Nuer) against the government dominated by northern Sudanese, and has raged with few significant breaks since Sudanese independence in 1955 (Daly and Sikainga 1993; Hutchinson 1996).

Tensions between north and south are rooted in cultural, as well as religious, differences. The north—which dominates the government of Sudan—is culturally a part of the Arab world and is predominantly Islamic (Deng 1995).

In contrast, southerners—such as the Nuer—belong culturally to sub-Saharan Africa. Many southerners have converted to Christianity in response to missionary efforts of the past half century; at the same time, indigenous religions based in animist and polytheistic belief systems remain important. Tensions between northern and southern Sudan are also linked to historical and contemporary inequalities between the two regions. In the early nineteenth century, when Sudan was ruled by the Turkish Ottoman empire, many areas of the south were subjected to intense slave raiding from the north. When Sudan came to be ruled through the joint Anglo-Egyptian Condominium in the late nineteenth century, economic development was confined largely to the north. Today there continues to be a pattern of economic exploitation of the south by the north. Moreover, recent government attempts to Islamicize Sudan, by imposing Islamic law and making Arabic the official language of the schools, have exacerbated tensions.

Over the last forty years intense fighting has broken out on several occasions. The phase of this conflict that led to the flight of the Nuer who have resettled in the United States began in the early 1980s, when the most important rebel group, the SPLA (Sudanese People's Liberation Army) made significant gains in taking military control of major portions of southern Sudan. This war devastated the lives of millions, who suffered death and displacement through direct conflict, general regional insecurity, and the destruction of their economic livelihood (Hutchinson 1996). Since the early 1980s, the United Nations High Commissioner for Refugees estimates that there have been as many as two millions deaths and four million people displaced from their homes to other areas of Sudan. Over half a million southern Sudanese are still international refugees. Only in 2005, with the signing of the Comprehensive Peace Agreement between the government of Sudan and the SPLA, has there been a hope of peace in southern Sudan, after 21 years of conflict. This has not brought peace and stability to all of southern Sudan, however, as war continues in the now much-publicized Darfur region in western Sudan, and much of the rest of the south continues to be plagued by insecurity caused by still-active militias and interethnic clashes (UNHCR 2006).

By the early 1990s, as many as half a million people had been displaced from southern Sudan and were living as refugees in southwestern Ethiopia. These included many Nuer, particularly from eastern Nuer tribes such as the Eastern Jikany, who had inhabited the border regions between the two countries. For several years many Nuer survived in camps in Ethiopia, sponsored by the United Nations High Commission for Refugees (UNHCR), but from 1991 to 1992 life in the camps was disrupted by the revolution in Ethiopia which caused chaos in many areas. Camps were closed, forcing many Nuer to assess their alternatives. Some sought to return to Sudan for at least a time, but insecurity remained a problem. Having lost all their livestock in the war, Sudan offered little opportunity for a secure and economically viable way of life. Many chose, instead, to move to new refugee camps in Kenya to the south. These not only offered the hope of safety, but also informed Nuer of programs in Kenya that could help refugees permanently resettle in a new country—Australia, Canada, or, most importantly, the United States.

While only a relatively small portion of the Nuer who wished to move to the United States were granted permission to do so, by 1994 significant numbers were entering this country. According to the Immigration and Naturalization Service (1997) by 1996, 3,888 Sudanese refugees (largely Nuer but also including other southern Sudanese) had been admitted to the United States. United States refugee agencies resettled the Nuer in upstate New York, San Diego, Nashville, and several cities in the midwest, such as Sioux Falls (South Dakota), Des Moines (Iowa), Omaha (Nebraska), and the metropolitan area of the Twin Cities of Minneapolis and St. Paul. Approximately 400 Nuer found their way to the Twin Cities in the 1990s. They were either sent there directly by religious or government agencies directing their resettlement, or went there later to rejoin friends and relatives after having been initially placed in another city. Sudanese refugees have continued to enter the United States up through the present. In 2001–2002, over 3,000, mostly young men, were admitted to the United States, when the United States committed to resettling the remaining "Lost Boys," youth who had been separated from their families in southern Sudan and lived for many years in refugee camps in northern Kenya.

THE CONTEXT OF FIELDWORK

I first learned that there were Nuer in Minnesota in late 1995 when I heard a report on Minnesota Public Radio describing the resettlement of Sudanese in the rather homogenous white northern suburbs of the Twin Cities. Aware of the Nuer's importance in the history of anthropology, I was fascinated to learn that they were now coming to America. I had only recently completed my doctoral fieldwork in Kenya among the Samburu, a people in many ways quite similar to the Nuer. Like the Nuer, the Samburu are pastoralists who survive predominantly through the herding of cattle. There are broad similarities in language and culture, and indeed the part of southern Sudan from which the Nuer in Minnesota originated and the area of northern Kenya where the Samburu live are separated only by about 200 miles. Both live in relatively remote, underdeveloped rural areas of their countries, with poor roads and few educational opportunities, and have relatively restricted knowledge of life outside their areas. Having seen firsthand the contrasts between life in rural East Africa and life in the United States—and struck by how unprepared my Samburu friends would be for life in the United States—I could not help but wonder what the Nuer were experiencing, uprooted and faced with starting over in a country so different from their own. I sought contact with the Nuer community in the hope of learning more about them and also to try to help in any way I could to ease their transition to life in the United States.

Over the next few months I became involved in the community in a number of ways. I helped organize a drive for household goods through a local church, met individually with families to discuss particular problems they were experiencing, and drove men to potential employers as they sought jobs. Later, I helped develop a mentoring/friendship program between Nuer and American youth which was funded through the Minneapolis Public Schools. I also became one of the American members of the Board of Trustees of the mutual assistance organization which the Nuer founded in Minnesota.

These activities of community development framed my research. As I worked with the Nuer in order to ease their adjustment to life in Minnesota, I began to learn informally about their lives, their culture, and their experiences. I got to know many Nuer, made friends in the community, and established good rapport through material and nonmaterial assistance. When later in 1996 I received a research grant from the Minnesota Historical Society to begin formal research through the documentation of Nuer experiences of displacement and resettlement, this followed in a relatively natural way from my other forms of involvement with the Nuer.

This project employed a variety of anthropological research methodologies and over time was broadened in scope and funding. Quantitative surveys were administered that aimed to create a fairly complete community profile, including information about age, gender, tribal and clan affiliation, education and work experiences, and basic outlines of the Nuer refugee experience. With many informants I followed the initial interview with more intensive research methods, such as life history research, in-depth structured interviews, and detailed case studies. Throughout the research, both participant observation and involvement in community development activities continued alongside more formal research methodologies. Since the main research period, I have continued to make brief research visits to Nuer friends and informants in order to track ongoing changes in the Nuer community.

2

Nuer Journeys: War, Flight, and Resettlement

The rebels had been coming to James Tap's village for some time. Situated only a few days' walk from the Ethiopian border, rebels controlled much of the area, and his village was on a major route which the rebels often took when launching attacks on government forces.

It was 1987 then, and James was a youth of about fourteen, having only recently been initiated into manhood with the six scars of *gaar* incised into his forehead. His father, the village chief, had found it necessary to provide the rebels with provisions to feed their army, such as cattle and maize. When another villager—perhaps jealous of the chief's position—reported to the government that the chief had been neglecting his position and aiding the rebels, soldiers were sent to arrest him. A skirmish ensued between the soldiers and the villagers, who did not want their chief arrested, and several villagers were wounded. James's father, however, was able to escape with his family, and they walked—without their cattle, which were taken by the government—to the camp at Itang on the Ethiopian border, sponsored by the United Nations High Commission for Refugees (UNHCR). After staying there several months, James's father heard reports from relatives that the government troops were no longer coming to their village. So he decided to return alone. No sooner had he returned, however, when someone (perhaps the new chief) reported that the former "traitorous chief" was back, and soldiers came to the village to arrest him. He was imprisoned in Nassir for three months before managing to escape and returned to his family in the refugee camp in Ethiopia. But beatings, deprivation, and unhygienic conditions had taken their toll, and he died before the year was over.

Thus began James's seven-year journey from a small village in rural Africa, across three countries and thousands of miles leading to resettlement in the United States. James's story, however dramatic it might be, is commonplace among the Nuer who have resettled in Minnesota. Every Nuer in Minnesota has endured war, famine, disease, and a host of other obstacles while successfully negotiating the vagaries of international politics to gain asylum in a new land. While refugees are often portrayed as helpless victims (women with small children form the most common media images of refugees), the Nuer have shown themselves to be fighters and survivors, who through unrelenting resolve and often ingenious strategies have struggled to forge a new life for themselves.

THE INTERNATIONAL REFUGEE PROBLEM

The twentieth century has been termed The Century of the Refugee (Cuno 1997: 114). War, famine, and political oppression have fueled the movement of people across national borders on a scale unprecedented in human history. Indeed, the Second World War alone resulted in the displacement of over forty million people. International law defines a refugee as someone who flees their country because of the real or potential threat of persecution based on their ethnic group, political views, or religious beliefs (Haines 1985). This definition serves to distinguish those fleeing persecution from economic migrants, who leave their countries or home areas primarily in order to flee economic hardship or to seek better opportunities elsewhere. These distinctions are, however, far from clear-cut. Economic problems frequently have political roots, and those officially defined as "refugees" may have a variety of reasons, including economic motivations, for seeking resettlement in a new country. In getting permission to resettle in the United States, the Nuer have had to prove that they are actually fleeing persecution and do not simply wish to come to the United States for other reasons.

In the contemporary world, the number of refugees remains high internationally, due to wars and internal conflicts, as well as political, economic, and ecological upheavals. The United States Commission for Refugees (USCR 2006) estimates that there are twelve million international refugees in the world today, as well as an additional 23 million internally displaced persons—people who have been driven from their homes but have remained within the borders of their own countries. As of 1997, southern Sudan was one of the world's "leaders" in refugees, with over 350,000 international refugees (mostly in Ethiopia, Kenya, Uganda, and Zaire). Today there are an estimated 700,000 refugees from Sudan, mainly hosted in neighboring countries, and between five and seven million internally displaced persons in Sudan.

THE WAR IN SOUTHERN SUDAN

"When elephants fight it is the grass that suffers."
African Proverb

War has dominated the lives of southern Sudanese for nearly half a century. Since independence from Great Britain in the late 1950s, armed conflict has been the principal medium to promote the divided visions which southerners and northerners have for the future of Africa's second largest nation (Deng 1995).

The divisions between south and north are serious and real, grounded in both current social, political, economic, and religious differences, as well as historical forces which have created both antipathy and inequality between south and north. In the nineteenth century, the Arab-dominated north saw the south principally as a raiding ground for slaves, ivory, and cattle; many northerners continue to view the south within this framework, as a resource to be exploited and a wilderness to be tamed (Deng 1995; Daly and Sikainga 1993). Politically and economically the north dominates the national scene, and has used this power at times to promote an Islamic agenda throughout the country, including the south which primarily follows Christianity and indigenous religions. The recent discovery of oil reserves in western areas of southern Sudan has added a very real economic basis to the conflict as well (Kok 1992).

In response to northern domination, southern groups have resorted to armed struggle on many occasions since independence. Going by names such as Anya Anya, Anya Anya II, the Sudanese People's Liberation Army, the Sudanese People's Liberation Movement, and the United Sudanese Democratic Front, southern rebel groups have pursued a variety of sometimes competing agendas in seeking to rectify the inequality between south and north (Hutchinson 1996). In some cases they have sought simply to create a more equal, united Sudan; in others they have sought greater autonomy, or even independence, for the south. The Comprehensive Peace Agreement (CPA), signed in 2005 by the Sudanese government and the main rebel groups, offers hope for a lasting peace that respects the autonomy and dignity of southerners such as the Nuer. War, however, continues in some areas of the south, particularly the Darfur region, while general conditions of insecurity persist throughout much of the south owing to interethnic fighting and the activities of still heavily armed militias.

Most southern Sudanese have, in principle, supported rebel movements against the government, seeing them as responses to true oppression which they have faced. Even in 1990, after years of war and famine, many Nuer and other southerners remained convinced that peace could only come if the terms were equitable. In the words of one Nuer man "The peace of a slave is not worth it!" (Hutchinson 1996: p. 9). Still, it is the southerners who suffer most directly. It is their homes that have become the battlefields, their fields which have been burned, and their herds which have been looted to feed the opposing armies. Their former, relatively quiet way of life based on subsistence agriculture and the herding of livestock has been irrevocably torn apart by civil war.

Survival in a war zone results in shifting loyalties, and villagers often find themselves pitted against the rebel army for their livelihood. Gatluak Luoth describes the predicament that many of the Nuer face as their homes become battlefields—if you side with the government, the rebels will kill you; if you side with the rebels, the government will kill you. Even if you seek to be neutral, one side will assume that your loyalty lies with whichever forces are dominant in your area. Both the government and the rebels are responsible for the destruction of Nuer villages. On one hand, government forces attack villages which they believe to be rebel strongholds. On the other hand, rebel forces often control the areas where the Nuer live; in the minds of many Nuer, the rebel forces are frequently more disruptive to the peace in their areas than the government.

Chuol Mut recalls life in the Maiwut area in the late 1980s. As a teenager of about sixteen, he joined his father, his brother, and other villagers to fight the rebels whose cause he otherwise supported. The crux of the conflict was the demand put on villagers by rebel forces, to feed their soldiers—demanding grain and livestock and looting cattle if these demands were not met. The Nuer from Chuol's village depended on the food for their survival and for the survival of their children, and found it necessary to take up arms to try to drive the rebels away from the village.

As the war became particularly intense in the late 1980s, life in Sudan became untenable for many Nuer. In some cases this was the result of a direct threat to their lives. Kun Buol's village, for example, was bombed by the government because of widespread rebel activity in the area. James Deng was suspected of being a rebel sympathizer by the government after he petitioned for the release from prison of other Nuer who had been accused of being rebels. The Nuer found in many cases that there was simply no way to survive in their home areas after their fields were burned and their cattle looted. Nyabuom Diew, for instance, retreated with her husband to another village in search of safety, but after a while food ran out and they left again, this time for a refugee camp. In still other cases, some stayed behind, while they sent children to live with family members in refugee camps, where they might be safe, fed, and perhaps have the opportunity to attend school.

There were a variety of options open to the Nuer within this brutal context, none of them particularly attractive. Some tried to remain, moving to a safer area within their region, eking out whatever meager existence was possible. This situation was particularly difficult for children whose parents were killed or who were separated from their parents in the war. Groups of 100 to 200 children wandered the countryside, surviving as they could on fish or other wild foods, earning the moniker "The Lost Boys of Sudan." Other Nuer decided to make the long and dangerous journey to the Sudanese capital of Khartoum in the north. Life in Khartoum meant poverty, victimization, and oppression, but at least there was peace. In 1990, 1.8 million southern Sudanese, many of them Nuer, lived in makeshift slums in garbage dumps or other previously uninhabited areas on the outskirts of Khartoum. They had no regular means to support themselves and were subject on a daily basis to racial, ethnic, and political oppression. Without national I.D. cards (which they were not issued because they had no address) they were subject to arbitrary arrest or worse—floggings and conscription into the national army, after which they might be sent back to the south to fight their fellow Nuer. These squatter camps were often bulldozed without a moment's notice by the government, which wanted to relocate the southerners to areas far from Khartoum (Hutchinson 1996).

Hutchinson (1992, 1996) has graphically described the difficult Nuer journeys to Khartoum, as well as the appalling conditions in the squatter camps. In 1990, she met many Nuer in Khartoum whom she had known in the south prior to the war. Gatcaar Biliu, a boy of about eleven, told Hutchinson how his life fell apart after his mother was murdered by government soldiers who tried to rape her at gunpoint. Eventually he reached Khartoum—but only after acting as a servant for Arab soldiers, working for a short time as a prostitute, and witnessing countless murders and mutilations of his fellow southerners. In Khartoum, he survived through begging. He slept outside, and had become addicted to sniffing glue and drinking benzine. Another man, Riak Kai, led a group of 117 Nuer on matted rafts to the regional city of Malakal. When their homes and fields had been burned by Arab militias—which had been armed by the government—disease and famine ravaged their area, and they resolved to flee on their perilous river journey. Braving disease, army boats, crocodiles, and hippopotamuses, only 87 of the original 117 reached Malakal alive. Riik Kai eventually got to Khartoum, only to be displaced once more when the government bulldozed his home.

The Nuer who found their way to Minnesota took a variety of paths. John Koang, a young man in his twenties, took one of the most unusual routes. Initially in the Sudanese army, he defected to the rebels and later went far afield in search of safety. He ended up in what he hoped would be a safe haven, Iraq—a distant, though not unheard of destination for Nuer migratory laborers (e.g., Hutchinson 1996: p. 56). Unfortunately, he arrived at an exceptionally bad time—shortly before the first Gulf War. With Iraq engulfed in war, he embarked on a long, circuitous journey through a variety of African countries—Chad, Nigeria—and even into Europe before eventually reaching the United States.

Peter Lual, a man in his forties had a very different kind of journey. Peter left Sudan earlier than most of the other Nuer in Minnesota, having fled in the 1970s during an earlier phase of the civil war. Even as a youngster, he recalls seeing soldiers travelling around his home area, harassing and beating people, until his family fled the area. They returned, but later, other fighting broke out, and Peter went to Khartoum for work and to avoid the war, and while there he also went to school. He left Khartoum because of discrimination from northerners—in one instance he was attacked on a bus—and went to Addis Ababa in Ethiopia because at the time fighting blocked the passage to his home area. After finishing secondary school he continued to live in Addis Ababa where he received refugee assistance from the UNHCR. When the revolution came to Addis Ababa, life became difficult and dangerous, with shooting in the streets. Worse yet, Peter was arrested and kept in prison for two years, after having been seen asking for assistance at a foreign embassy. In prison he was badly beaten and his health suffered. Eventually he was granted the opportunity to resettle in the United States at the initiative of the UNHCR.

The most common route, however, for the Nuer who eventually reached Minnesota was through Itang refugee camp, run by the UNHCR, just across the border in neighboring Ethiopia. Like 400,000 other southerners, many Nuer "followed the trail of [human] bones eastward" (Hutchinson 1996: p. 6) to the relative safety of Ethiopian camps. Because the Nuer in Minnesota come overwhelmingly from southeastern Sudan, Itang was a relatively short trip, usually requiring a walk of three to ten days.

There were both positive and negative things about these camps, and reactions to life in the camps varied considerably. James Tap's reaction is representative of many Nuer refugees, who found the camps unpleasant, but the only opportunity for relative safety.

> . . . I cannot say that it was good because at that time it was really very bad. . . . There was not any good education. Even there was not enough food and also there was no good hospital to take care of us.

Certainly conditions were difficult, with tens of thousands of refugees living in tents, in close proximity to one another. Food was generally available, since the UNHCR provided relief food, but it was unappealing fare which had the sole purpose of keeping people alive—a monotonous diet of grain sent by international donors. Milk, a staple of the Nuer diet, and considered to be the most perfect food, was generally unavailable at the camps, as were meat, vegetables, and many other foods to which the Nuer were accustomed. Traditional ceremonies and recreational activities, such as dancing, were also not easy to perform in the camps. Further, in the crowded camp conditions disease was rampant and medical facilities were inadequate to meet the overwhelming need. Physical security also remained an issue. Fighting sometimes erupted between different ethnic groups occupying the camps and the presence of rebel forces could also be disruptive. The area in which the camp was located was controlled by Sudanese rebels, and they sometimes tried to force youth to join their army or sent them off to collect firewood or do other kinds of menial work for them.

Life in the camps, in sum, was far from easy. Compared with the areas from which they were coming, however, food was much more plentiful, and there was much less threat of violence. And while there were no schools at Itang, educational opportunities were available in other camps, a fact which some Nuer men cite as an inducement when weighing the decision to abandon their home areas. From Itang some young men, including James Tap, took the opportunity to relocate to another camp at Dimma, approximately 50 miles further into Ethiopia, where they were able to attend school.

In the early 1990s, the Nuer's tenuous refuge in southwestern Ethiopia was itself thrown into chaos, as civil war elsewhere in Ethiopia resulted in the overthrow of the socialist regime of Marium Haile Mengistu, who had ruled Ethiopia since deposing Emperor Haile Selassie in the 1970s. The camps were closed, and most Nuer refugees fled for a time across the border to rebel-controlled areas of Sudan. There they faced famine and other hardships because there were no facilities in place to serve their needs. When order returned to Ethiopia, the camps were reopened, but the living conditions were worse than before, and supplies of food and medicine were inadequate. Fighting also ensued with another Sudanese ethnic group occupying the camp, the Annuak (Uduk), resulting in the deaths of many Nuer (see also James 1997).

At about the same time, news began to spread of refugee camps in Kenya from a handful of the Nuer who had already gone there. The new camps offered a place of safety, away from the deteriorating situation in Ethiopia and continuing troubles in their own country. More importantly, many had heard of the possibility, once in Kenya, of getting permission to resettle in a third country, particularly the United States or Canada. From the little they might have heard on the radio, from a few foreigners they had met, or from a handful of the Nuer who had already reached the United States, they concluded that the United States offered hope for a better life. Food and health care, they heard, were readily available in the United States; there was no war; and there was the possibility of getting both an education and a good job. As a result, tens of thousands of Nuer embarked on another journey, this time a few hundred miles to the south to Walda refugee camp in northern Kenya.

THE CAMPS IN KENYA

How does a refugee travel several hundred miles and cross the border into another country? Getting from one place to another with relative ease is such an integral part of contemporary American life that it may be difficult to imagine things any other way. If an American needs to get to another city, he or she merely gets in a car, hops on a bus or a train or a plane, and goes. Even going to another country is not a major problem, with easy access to passports and travel documents at the local government service center. Yet it was not so easy for the Nuer who had little or no money, and no means to get the passports and visas required to travel legally.

With no cattle and no employment, raising even the small amount of cash to travel to Kenya by public transportation was often problematic. Nyadaar Chay, a young woman in her twenties, travelled with her husband and small children to Kenya in 1992. They employed an unusual and innovative strategy to raise the money to get to Kenya—selling the tent which they had been issued by the UNHCR to local Ethiopians. Another women, Nyakat Dung, raised money by collecting firewood in the forest and selling it to local Ethiopians; she also sold a portion of the relief food supplied by the UNHCR, or sometimes brewed the grain into beer and sold that.

For some, like James Tap, the issue of money was not a major obstacle. He had been receiving a small student stipend from the UNHCR while he pursued his secondary education at Dimma in Ethiopia, and he was able to use this to pay his fare on a truck to the Kenyan border. Once there, however, James faced other problems. Travelling to Kenya was illegal. Like other Nuer, James had no passport and no entrance visa from the Kenyan embassy in Addis Ababa. In order to cross the border, Nuer normally went on foot through the mountainous terrain in the border area. Often there were no problems, and they successfully crossed and made their way to the refugee camp at Walda. Sometimes, however, they were caught by the Kenyan police, and had to pay a bribe or else be arrested. James and a young man with whom he was travelling were caught and imprisoned for two weeks. At the trial the judge initially planned to send them to Kokoma—a camp on the small strip of land which formed the Kenya–Sudan border—with the aim of deporting them to Sudan. They pleaded not to be sent there because the area is remote and dangerous and they had no desire to be sent back to Sudan. Also, Kokoma had no program for resettlement in the United States, which was James's ultimate goal. The judge relented and sent them instead to Walda refugee camp, where most of the Nuer refugees in Kenya were then residing.

Walda itself, however, proved to be a dangerous place. In the crowded conditions of the camp, tensions quickly arose between the Nuer and the Gaari, a group of Muslim refugees from Ethiopia who (unlike the Nuer) had brought guns to Kenya. Two Nuer men were murdered by the Gaari when they strayed from camp, their genitals were cut off, and their bodies hung in trees. When the Nuer went outside the camp to bury their dead, the Gaari returned and taunted them about the others they would soon kill. The Nuer took up the challenge, and with sticks and other implements attacked the well-armed Gaari. In the ensuing fight, five Nuer were killed before the Kenya police intervened.

James did not stay long at Walda but soon left, travelling illegally with a friend. He had heard that the UNHCR wanted to send all the Nuer to the camp at Kokoma—something he had avoided once and now wanted to avoid again. He decided to try to make his way to another camp a thousand miles away at Thika, a small city near Nairobi. From there he and his friend hoped to get permission to resettle in the United States.

Once again, however, James ended up in jail. At a police checkpoint all the passengers on the truck James was travelling in were required to get off and present their Kenyan I.D., and James was caught. His scars of *gaar* and lack of knowledge of Kiswahili (the Kenyan national language) made him stand out in the crowd, and he did not, of course, have a Kenyan I.D., or any of the appropriate documents, since he was travelling illegally. He was recognized as a foreigner, arrested, and sent to jail.

James and his friend spent three months in jail. On release, they were able to make their way to another camp, called Iffo, that James learned had been the destination to which the

Nuer he had left in Walda were transferred after the fight with the Gaari. At Iffo, applications were being taken to apply for resettlement in the United States. Once there, James quickly began the process of getting permission to resettle.

APPLYING FOR RESETTLEMENT

Applying for permission to resettle was a trying process for most Nuer. First, there was the screening interview, conducted to establish whether an individual met the established criteria for being granted the status of "refugee." On the face of it, this may seem like a relatively innocuous process—simply providing information about yourself and your experiences. Yet the nature of the information, the context of the interview, and the consequences of failure made this an extraordinarily stressful experience for many of the Nuer.

Try to imagine yourself in a foreign country, being interviewed by people whose language you have never heard, and communicating through a translator whose abilities may be less than perfect. You are asked a long series of complex and difficult questions, which the interviewer requires you to answer in very specific ways. If there are any inconsistencies, you will be presumed to be lying and you will not pass. If your body language or your style of speech suggests that you are lying you also may not pass. You know that very specific answers are required, but you may not know what those specific answers are, and those answers may, in fact, not reflect the exact truth of your own situation. Yet after years of suffering through famine and death, in a war zone and in refugee camps, your entire future depends on your ability to answer these questions to the satisfaction of the interviewer. Not surprisingly, most of the Nuer describe the resettlement interview as having been among the worst parts of the process of resettlement.

Even getting to the interview stage was trying. For those who already had family in the United States—most commonly, brothers—the process was the least difficult. Their relatives would send an "affidavit of relationship," which allowed for family reunification in the United States. Although there was no guarantee of an interview being scheduled quickly, they were given a higher priority for being interviewed. Others were less fortunate. They simply filled out information sheets, and then waited months or sometimes years to see if they would be interviewed. The resettlement agencies visited Iffo three times before James was given a screening interview. Often, by the time an application was processed, the person selected for a screening interview may have already given up hope for resettlement and decided to go elsewhere. In some cases the person had already been successfully resettled in a different country, such as Canada or Australia. Families and friends would make certain that the opportunity to be interviewed was not wasted, and they often selected an alternate to be interviewed in the applicant's place. Lacking any form of positive identification, it was generally quite easy to make such substitutions.

Once in the interview, it was necessary to provide comprehensive information on family and background. Many of the Nuer found this to be difficult because of their large families and because they had not seen some relatives for many years. They had trouble providing exact ages since few of the Nuer from rural villages know the year and date of their birth. Although the Nuer had difficulties providing this information, their accounts needed to appear complete and consistent, or they could be denied resettlement. Then there was the critical part of the interview: explaining their reason for leaving Sudan. Simply having your country devastated by war was not enough. The Immigration and Naturalization Service (INS) defines a refugee in a very specific way:

> A refugee is an alien outside the United States who is unable or unwilling to return to his or her country because of well-founded fear of persecution. Claims of persecution must be based on race, religion, nationality, membership in a particular social group or political opinion (INS 1996: p. 72).

Based on this definition, it was necessary to demonstrate the ways in which the situation in their country had affected them individually. Often this meant that the Nuer had to show that they faced persecution from their role in the government, or that they or their family were subjected to direct personal danger. These requirements were hard to understand and seemed arbitrary, even perverse, to the Nuer. They had all suffered as a result of the ravages of war and famine, and did not see that having suffered in one way or in another should dictate that one person had the right to go to the United States while another was forced to stay behind. Their reasons for fleeing were commonsensical ones—if you saw your neighbor killed by soldiers you would not wait for them to come and kill you—yet such a reason would be inadequate under INS guidelines.

As they learned what the interviewers wanted to hear, the Nuer felt compelled to alter their stories accordingly. Gatluak Luoth, for example—who had fled Sudan because of general conditions of warfare and famine—explained how he had altered his story in order to gain resettlement. "I told them that the soldiers killed my father, and then my mother, and then they were looking for me." When Gatluak said this to me, his brother laughed and exclaimed, "You cannot fail the interview if you tell them that." Another Nuer described how he had failed the screening interview the first time, when he said, truthfully, that he had come to the refugee camp in Ethiopia to get medical assistance for his sick child. When he later managed to get a second interview, he was accepted for resettlement by making up a story which purported to describe his personal persecution. "It's funny that when you tell them the truth," he noted, "they can't accept you."

In February 1994, six years after having left home and two years after having come to Kenya, James Tap finally received notification that he had been accepted for resettlement in the United States. He was then brought to Nairobi for the final steps prior to resettlement. Life in Nairobi was difficult. James, like other Nuer, lived in a tented camp on the outskirts of the city. It was the rainy season, when Nairobi experiences its coldest seasonal temperatures. Rain came into the tents at night, sometimes causing miserable conditions. In Nairobi, James was issued travel documents, went through a brief orientation course in American culture, and was given a medical check—the final hurdle to pass before being given final permission to resettle.

James passed his medical check, but many others did not. Among the most common reasons for failure was infection with H.I.V., the AIDS virus. AIDS is not common in rural Nuer villages, but being refugees made the Nuer increasingly vulnerable. Some had gone to cities such as Nairobi and Addis Ababa where the disease is common, and then returned to refugee camps and spread the disease. The final moments of jubilation could quickly, then, turn to despair. So it was for Nyadaar Chay's husband, who learned at the last minute that he was infected and could not travel with his wife and family to the United States.

In July of 1994, James boarded the plane which would take him to the United States. Unlike most of the Nuer, James had actually flown in a plane once before, having travelled by a small aircraft from Dimma camp to Addis Ababa. Many Nuer, however, were terrified that the *rianhial*—sky boat—would fall from the air, and they found the flight almost impossible to endure. For these refugees from rural Africa the plane trip was a sudden and dramatic entrance to the industrialized world—and one which would bring them to many other new and strange experiences in a new land.

3

The Birth of a Community

I say "What is that?" because . . . there is white, white, every-where on the trees, the house, everywhere on the house. I don't see grass. I don't see the trees very well. I wonder what happened to the tree. And there was one guy who picked us up in the airport and he said "That is called snow." When we get out: Ohhhhhh! Whooaaa! Terrible. And then they brought out big jackets and I said "What do we do with this?" They said "Outside it is very cold. You can wear it." I say "Okay." I am not sure. When I get out I say, I say, "Oh. That makes a change." That is my first change when I came.

Nuer man, describing first impressions
at Sioux Falls Airport, South Dakota

The move to the United States was a shock for Nuer refugees who had never been outside of rural Africa, had seen few images of this country, and had never experienced any weather other than the equatorial heat of Sudan, Ethiopia, and Kenya. "How do people live?" was the reaction of one young Nuer man when he saw snow on landing at New York's JFK Airport.

Adjusting to changes in the physical environment was, however, in many ways the easy part. Housing, transportation, work—in fact, virtually all aspects of life—bore little resemblance to the Nuer's familiar way of life. In the earliest days, even the simplest tasks—how to shop or how to cook—seemed like insurmountable challenges. Beyond changes in daily routines, there was the necessity to reforge their social worlds. In Sudan, and even in the refugee camps, the Nuer lived within a network of family and friends which made up a close-knit community. Suddenly, in America they were unusual, and often isolated, strangers.

GETTING STARTED IN THE UNITED STATES

To most Nuer, life in the United States was, at the beginning, strange but largely positive. After conditions in the refugee camps, they were happy to be in a place where problems of day-to-day survival were no longer an issue, where food was plentiful, where medical care was available, and where there was no war. At the same time, virtually every aspect of daily life was completely different from anything which they knew. Although some men had had at least brief experiences in African cities—working in Khartoum or going to Addis Ababa to study—for most Nuer this was their first significant time outside of rural Africa. Along with the frigid cold of Minnesota, and other northern areas of Nuer resettlement, basic aspects of everyday living were completely unfamiliar.

For many, the resettlement process involved either an intentional or inadvertent change in identity as well. Nuer names typically have some social significance. For instance, a person born around the time a new *luak* (cattle byre) was built might be Nyaluak (for a girl) or Gatluak (for a boy). The name Chuol is given to a child whose older sibling has died; that Chuol is the most common male name in Minnesota is testimony to the struggles the Nuer have endured. In Africa, some were required to take Christian names like James, Peter, or Paul when they converted to Christianity. As the Nuer gained permission to resettle, however, their names were frequently changed. Sometimes this was intentional, in order to assume the identity of an absent person who had been granted a resettlement interview. Other times, a bureaucratic mistake mixed up someone's first, last, and middle name. In other cases, a friend or relative inadvertently put a nickname rather than a person's true name on an affidavit of relationship, forcing them to accept the new name or stay behind. As a result, many of the Nuer sought to have their names legally changed to the correct one soon after arriving in the United States.

All of the Nuer had someone to lend them at least some minimal assistance in getting started. If relatives were already living in the United States, they would be there to greet the newcomers, provide temporary housing, and supply some basic knowledge of how to function in the United States. A dozen or more people sometimes lived in a two-bedroom

Snow and cold were a shock to many Nuer who had never lived outside of tropical Africa before coming to Minnesota.

apartment during the weeks or months in which the new arrivals were getting adjusted. In other cases, American sponsors helped the Nuer get started in the United States; they picked them up at the airport, brought them to some type of housing, and tried to aid in the adjustment process. The sponsors' level of commitment varied widely. While sponsorship sometimes led to serious commitments of several months or more in helping a refugee family, in other cases help ended very soon after resettlement.

Dak Lut's description of his first day in the United States—in early 1994—illustrates how strange the experience could be and the unexpected difficulties a new arrival could encounter. With his wife and daughter, Dak was brought from the airport to an apartment by their sponsor, who made an effort to ensure that they had everything they needed. The sponsor took them through the apartment's bathroom, showing them the toilet, the toilet paper, the toothpaste, and the toothbrushes. He showed them how to operate the lights and pointed out various aspects of the kitchen, including the location of the meat, vegetables, sugar, and rice, and how the stove worked. All of this was a lot to take in. "When she left," Dak recalled, "We forgot all. When we tried to cook, ooohhhh . . . we get [a] terrible thing."

Dak and his wife did not remember how to turn on the stove, and the family did not eat for most of the day. After a few hours, an American who lived in the apartment building came up to see how they were doing—but this unfortunately did not improve the situation.

"Then one American came down and he came to visit us," Dak explained, "And he says, 'How are you? You are coming to America?' We say, 'Yes.' He said, 'Can I help you?'" While relating this, Dak let out an exaggerated gasp—"Ohhhhhhh"—and smiled. "When we were in orientation, there was one lady who told us that if someone comes and says, 'Can I help you?' say, 'No.' If you don't know her or him very well, don't allow him to do something for you."

Hungry and unable to cook, Dak refused the offer of assistance because of warnings in the cultural orientation programs in Nairobi that some people in America may offer to help in order to take advantage of you or rob you. Dak and his family stayed in the apartment, helpless for several more hours. Finally, the neighbor—perhaps sensing trouble—returned bearing a Bible in order to show his good intent. With that symbol in hand, Dak decided to let him in, and the neighbor assisted him in cooking.

However small or dramatic the adjustments, most of the Nuer have adapted fairly quickly to the basic facets of everyday American life. Dak, for instance, recounted his disastrous cooking story to me three years after the fact, while I ate rice and stew which his wife had prepared on the stove, and which Dak himself had reheated in the microwave. Their experiences in Africa—coping with war and moving from one camp to another, and from one country to another—have taught them to adapt to change quickly. Indeed, those who made it to the United States are, perhaps, those most ready to face the challenges of a new life, for they had to be resourceful and determined to get here.

PATTERNS OF RESETTLEMENT

The major wave of resettlement in Minnesota began in November of 1994. While there had been some Nuer in Minnesota prior to this time, they had been relatively few and had largely escaped the notice of the host community. At the end of 1994, however, the Nuer began to arrive in unprecedented numbers, both as primary resettlees and as secondary migrants from other American cities. The precise number of Nuer is difficult to gauge, and indeed is in constant flux. While new arrivals continue to come to the Twin Cities from Africa or other states, other Nuer have moved elsewhere. At its largest, the Twin Cities community numbered perhaps 400; since 1997, migration to Iowa, South Dakota, and, in particular, Nebraska, has lowered the figure closer to 200 individuals.

Where a Nuer refugee initially resettled was generally not under his or her control. Those whose relatives sponsored them were sent to join them in the same community. For others, however, their placement was selected by resettlement agencies, based on criteria which were unknown to the refugees themselves. Sometimes this involved sending the Nuer to cities where individuals or organizations had volunteered to serve as sponsors in the initial period of resettlement. The general effect was to disperse the Nuer fairly widely in a number of communities with small numbers of Nuer.

In fact, since the 1960s the U.S. government has deliberately sought to disperse refugee populations and avoid what happened in the resettlement of Cuban refugees following the Communist takeover in Cuba (Haines 1982; Koltyk 1998). Cuban refugees settled primarily in Miami, and this had a major effect in changing the character of the city. Now government policy aims to avoid concentrations of refugee populations through dispersed resettlement.

Yet despite government policy, dispersed refugee populations have a tendency, after initial resettlement, to cluster together. Refugees are legal immigrants who receive permanent residency status; they are afforded most of the rights of citizens and can move freely like other Americans. After the first few months of being placed in one location, many refugees choose to move to join friends, relatives, and other members of their ethnic group. Consequently, dispersal is frequently a short-lived phenomenon; many refugee groups, such as the Hmong (Haines 1982; Koltyk 1998), have quickly formed large resettlement communities through secondary migration soon after initial resettlement.

Nuer experiences of resettlement have generally corresponded to this pattern. The Nuer in Minnesota had initially been resettled in a wide range of communities throughout the United States including Rochester, New York; Nashville, Tennessee; St. Louis, Missouri; Des Moines, Iowa; Cedar Falls, Iowa; Sioux Falls, South Dakota; Salt Lake City, Utah; and San Diego, California. Often within months, or even weeks, these refugees pulled up roots and came to Minnesota.

Why Minnesota? In comparison to other areas of the country, wages and availability of employment are relatively good. James Tap, for instance, enjoyed living in Houston, Texas during his brief stay there and especially liked the climate, which he found to be similar to Sudan. But the only job he was able to find paid between $4.00 and $5.00 per hour. Other Nuer found well-paying jobs in their initial location but sometimes found other opportunities to be lacking, particularly in education. Sometimes the jobs they were able to get made it difficult, or impossible, to go to school. In Sioux Falls, South Dakota, Dak Lut found it hard to work the late shift at a meat packing plant and also attend classes:

> I went to work at 2:30 at John Morrell and came back at 12 o'clock [midnight]. We have a lot of equipment to take off and so we lose one hour. . . . Then when you get home, you better put your dirty clothes in the laundry first. You need to go to the bathroom and wash yourself, because you get a lot of blood on your body. You wash yourself, and around three o'clock you can go to sleep. At three o'clock you will sleep. If you have school in the morning, at eight o'clock, that is not enough. You will be tired, tired, tired, yeah. I decided that I couldn't go to work and go to school. That is why I came here to Minneapolis.

Life in Minnesota promised to be much easier. Dak and his family were placed on public assistance, and Dak was able to pursue his studies. Although in his mid-twenties, Dak's immigration documents said he was several years younger, and he was thus allowed to enroll in high school. It was not simply that educational opportunities were better in Minnesota. Welfare benefits and requirements were also an issue. In Sioux Falls, Dak was not allowed to collect welfare as a full-time student, while in Minnesota he was allowed to do so.

Other factors also influenced the Nuer in deciding to move to Minnesota. One was the sheer number of Nuer already there. While some cities received substantial numbers of Nuer refugees (and continue to have many Nuer), others had only a handful. Living in a community with only a few Nuer was isolating and difficult, particularly given the low level of English competence which most Nuer had on arrival in the United States. The greater concentration of Nuer in Minnesota meant more people spoke their mother tongue, and there was also a greater likelihood of finding bilingual Nuer to serve as interpreters. Most importantly, however, it meant an end to loneliness, which was a major problem for many Nuer in the earliest stages of resettlement. Nyagoa Khot was a young wife with no children when she came to the United States by herself, after her husband failed the medical check. Settling first in upstate New York, she was isolated and depressed to be living in a place with few other Nuer and without her husband, who subsequently died while he was still in Kenya. Nyagoa Khot decided to travel to Sioux Falls where there were many more Nuer. There she met another man, whom she married, and they later moved together to Minnesota, where she was reunited with friends she had known in the refugee camps. Chuol Mut similarly notes:

> I have a lot of cousins here, lot of friends in Minnesota, so I don't enjoy Rochester [New York]. I just come here to get my friends and someone I like to talk to.

Some Nuer came to Minnesota simply because all their other friends were coming. When James Tap, for instance, left Texas to seek a better paying job, he first settled in Iowa, which he found to be a good location because there were many Nuer and reasonable job opportunities. But then, other Nuer decided to move to Minnesota. "I left Des Moines," he explained "because some of my friends, they plan to come here, and they were my roommates. There was no one who I could share a room with then."

The secondary migration of Nuer refugees has, in fact, taken on a dynamic of its own. As long-term refugees, the Nuer have developed an attentiveness to opportunities that can better their situation, and they have become accustomed to moving from place to place to improve their lot. Most of the Nuer in Minnesota made decisions to leave places not once, but many times, before coming to the United States—to leave the village for the refugee camp, perhaps to leave that camp for another where schooling was available, back to Sudan when war came to Ethiopia, then to Kenya when they heard of the possibility of resettlement, and eventually to the United States. To move from one place to another in pursuit of better opportunities has been a method of survival for Nuer refugees for over a decade—to continue to do so, then, has perhaps become a normal way of life for many Nuer.

Interestingly, communities wax and wane in their popularity as sites for secondary migration. In 1995, Minnesota was known among Nuer refugees nationally as a hot spot, a place where many Nuer were contemplating relocating. In early 1997, a similar phenomenon occurred with Omaha, Nebraska, and many Nuer in Minnesota relocated there. As a site gains prominence as a point for resettlement, it becomes a topic for active discussion. And as more and more people move, the process gains momentum as others decide to stay or follow.

NUER IN MINNESOTA: AN OVERVIEW

The Nuer are spread throughout the northern and central Twin Cities metropolitan area, without major residential concentrations. Initially most families settled in the northern outer ring suburbs—about 30 minutes from downtown Minneapolis—but later became somewhat more dispersed throughout the Twin Cities. Although it is not uncommon for two or three families to live fairly closely together—and Nuer express a desire to live close to one another—a scarcity of affordable housing in the suburbs makes it difficult for the Nuer to get apartments near one another. The result is that, at least so far, groups of families have not significantly clustered in the same apartment buildings or even in the same neighborhoods.

Low English competence and low education are characteristic of most Minnesota Nuer. Most men arrived knowing some English and have at least a functional vocabulary. Many had at least some schooling in Africa, particularly in refugee camps in Ethiopia. Still, even as their English skills improve, only a minority approach fluency. As for women, only one or two had attended any school at all before coming to the United States. As a result, most came without any knowledge of English or an ability to read (even in Nuer), and they have been slow to gain English language and literacy skills in the United States.

The population is comprised mostly of younger people. There are very few individuals older than their mid-thirties, and most are considerably younger. Most commonly, they live in young families, consisting of a husband, wife, and their young children. Dak Lut, for example, was one of the earliest Nuer arrivals in the Midwest, arriving with his family in Sioux Falls, South Dakota in 1994 and later moving to Minnesota for educational opportunities. His wife, Nyaluak, and their two children live together in a two-bedroom apartment. At times, an adult cousin has stayed with them, as well.

Unlike many refugee and immigrant populations in the United States, multigenerational families are unknown among the Nuer in Minnesota. Almost no members of the grandparent generation are around. The physical challenges involved in reaching refugee camps in Ethiopia and the multiple moves across national borders before eventual resettlement discouraged older Nuer from emigrating. Perhaps more important, older Nuer were reluctant to leave their homes and to abandon hope of returning there. The Nuer consider new adventures and new experiences to be the purview of the young, not something which would normally be of interest to older people. Further, there is the idea that their home, their "place," should not be abandoned, regardless of the problems faced there. Consequently, while older Nuer enthusiastically supported their children's efforts to seek safety and new opportunities in the United States, they considered it important, as well, that some people should remain to watch over and occupy (or in the future, reoccupy) their home area.

In addition to young families, there are significant numbers of single males, usually in their late teens to mid-twenties. These young men successfully applied for resettlement in the United States before they had the opportunity to get married and in some cases while they were still minors. Sometimes they live temporarily with the families of married friends or relatives, but more typically young men live together in groups of four or five, sharing living expenses while they work or go to school. Usually some of the men who live together are related—for instance as distant cousins—though unrelated friends are often included, as well.

Both Chut's living situation is typical of that of many young, unmarried Nuer men. About 22 years old, he shares an apartment with three cousins and friends who range in age from 19 to 24. Down the hall in their apartment building is a similar group of young Nuer men. All of them had fled

Sudan as teenagers without their parents, and after many years in refugee camps eventually resettled in the United States. Some had resettled in other states before moving to Minnesota for school, employment, or just to join their friends. Living together provides sociability and allows them to share living expenses as they work or go to school. Were they in Sudan, these young men would have spent a great deal of time with one another as members of an age set in which they had been initated together. In Africa, age sets frequently form the basis for social life and shared living arrangements as young men migrate to cities (e.g., Mayer 1971). The lifestyle of Both and his friends is also not unlike that of American college students or other young people. In the living room there is a big TV, on which someone is usually channel surfing; athletic and weight equipment are strewn casually about the living room; and there are frequent visitors—most often Nuer, but also sometimes Americans whom they have met in school. Some young Nuer men have taken American nicknames which make their names easier to understand to American friends. I was surprised to find young men I knew as Mut and Bol answering the phone with names like "Mike" and "Jackson" and even suddenly referring to each other in this way. Besides helping to communicate with young Americans, the practice of nicknaming is also a kind of game younger Nuer started while living in the camps.

There are virtually no single adult women in the Minnesota Nuer community. In Africa, the Nuer considered it normal for a young man or male teenager to travel alone or with friends to refugee camps, but it was not culturally acceptable for a woman to do so. Such a journey would have posed considerable danger, particularly because Nuer women do not own or use weapons. Moreover, any girl or woman old enough to undertake such a journey would likely already have had a husband because Nuer girls are considered to be marriageable by their mid-teens.

There are some married women who are living without their husbands in Minnesota. Nyadaar Chay traveled with her husband as far as the refugee camps in Kenya, having left a camp in Ethiopia after the destruction caused by the overthrow of the Mengistu regime in 1991–1992. Her husband had heard about the opportunity to apply for resettlement in the United States, and they traveled together with their children to Kenya in order to seek permission to resettle. They successfully went through the interview process to gain permission to move to the United States, but serious problems developed shortly thereafter. Her husband failed the medical examination required of refugees and was denied permission to emigrate. She agreed, with extreme apprehension, to follow her husband's wishes and travel with their three children to the United States without him. The choice was a difficult one, but her husband felt that emigration presented the best opportunity for her and their children, and she eventually acquiesced. He now lives in the Ethiopian capital, Addis Ababa, and they remain hopeful that he will be given permission to join his family in the United States.

The death of a husband at a refugee camp or during the various travels in Africa may also result in a woman resettling alone with her children. Some unions have also dissolved in the United States. However, widowed, divorced, or separated women typically have a number of suitors and are likely to remarry fairly quickly. This process is not atypical of traditional Nuer culture, although there are many differences in what happens to widows in Sudan and the United States. As will be discussed in more detail in Chapter 5, marriage in Sudan involves a much broader kinship group beyond the nuclear family, so that a widow there would normally remain a part of her husband's family even after his death, with her subsequent children sired by his brother or other male kin. This kinship network is largely absent in the United States. Here the skewed gender ratio—a good number of young Nuer men seeking wives, but few marriageable Nuer women—is a substantial impetus towards remarriage.

The Nuer do their best to remain in contact with those they have left behind in Africa. Everyone has relatives remaining in camps in Ethiopia or Kenya, and most also have relatives still in Sudan. Ties to kin in Africa are important for many reasons. Beyond the obvious personal bonds, relatives in Africa are often dependent on remittances from the United States for their livelihood, and some are hoping to come to the United States. Moreover, some Nuer in Minnesota direct friends or relatives in Africa to perform culturally important duties for them in their absence. Contact is often maintained through letter writing—even the illiterate find someone to read or write a letter for them—and sometimes letters are composed in the form of cassette tapes. Sometimes relatives in Africa travel to a city—most commonly Addis Ababa—for the express purpose of telephoning the United States. The Nuer highly value these phone calls as a means of hearing news, managing affairs across vast distances, and keeping alive their social networks. At the same time, the cost of such calls can be extremely expensive. The Nuer sometimes have had their phones disconnected after being unable to pay their bill for international calls.

BECOMING A "COMMUNITY"

In recent years "community" has become one of the most overused words in contemporary English, such that people have come to ask what a community really is. Virtually any group of people has come to be called a "community" based on some shared characteristic. And yet, while it is easy to label someone a member of "The Gay Community" or "The African-American Community," there is more to a community than simply shared characteristics or affiliations. In contrast to this common usage, community implies something more mutual, more interactive as people live together, associate with one another, and are tied up in each other's lives in both symbolic and concrete ways. There are common activities and some sense of common purpose.

In what ways are the Nuer in Minnesota a community? Although they share Nuer ethnicity, as well as a wide range of similar experiences from their lives as refugees, the intricate community organization of Nuer life in Sudan has been wholly disrupted through the process of flight and resettlement. Many Nuer have few if any kin in Minnesota, and people come from different villages, different regions, and even different tribes within the broad Nuer ethnicity. A critical issue is, then, the extent to which—and how—Nuer refugees can come together to form a community.

THE BASIS OF NUER COMMUNITY IN SUDAN

The Nuer community in Sudan is based most centrally on kinship relationships. Two principal kinds of kinship relationship fuse together Nuer groups and individuals. The first, *mar*, describes an actual kinship relationship between individuals which can be directly traced through a line of relatives. Brothers, sisters, parents, uncles, aunts, and cousins are all *mar*. The second type of relationship is known as *buth*. *Buth* refers to relationships between lineages though actual links between individuals cannot be traced. (Evans-Pritchard 1951). A Nuer man, for instance, might consider himself to be a member of a lineage which traces descent from Dak, while another traces descent from Kuany. If there is believed to have been some type of relationship between Dak and Kuany, the members of the two lineages are said to be related through *buth*, although the actual links cannot be traced. This type of relationship is fundamental to the tribal organization of the Nuer, particularly in regard to alliances and warfare.

Any Nuer who share a relationship based on *mar* or *buth* are considered to be related. Others are considered to be *rul*, or strangers. In traditional life, however, all Nuer are able to trace some kind of kinship relationship with any other Nuer—whether through the intimate ties of the immediate family, through more distant relatives, through marriage, or even through a forefather or foremother from the earliest beginnings of Nuer mythology. Within a village, kinship ties are close and direct, while ties with those outside of the immediate circle of frequent contact are often more distant. Both kinds of ties, however, are crucial to any interaction within the traditional context. Rights, responsibilities, and proper conduct are all defined through the idiom of kinship, so that it is impossible to understand how to behave towards another Nuer without knowing the kinship relationship between you (Evans-Pritchard 1951).

The Nuer word *cieng* is the term most commonly used for "community." Usually *cieng* refers to the village itself, but it can also be used to refer to one's home area more generally. Even in the traditional context people frequently left their home areas for periods of time; men generally returned to the home village while women commonly stayed in their husband's village. The closest ties within the village are between the members of families, composed of a man, one or more wives, and their children. This unit is termed *gol* and refers to the dung hearth-fire at the center of the cattle byre which serves as the real and symbolic center of the homestead. All Nuer in the *cieng* are *jinmarida*—people linked through kinship relations (*mar*)—of one kind or another. Individuals are related in a variety of ways— through direct, traceable lines of kinship, through marriage, or through a shared kinship relation to a third person—but all village members are linked together in a web of kinship (Evans-Pritchard 1951).

Kinship, thus, plays an important role in forming a sense of community within Nuer villages in Sudan. Of additional importance is the solidarity expressed through mutual participation in wide-ranging economic and social activities, as well as shared economic and political interests. Farming lands, fishing grounds, water supplies, and grazing areas all belong to the village. Young men go together to community-wide dances in war lines (*dep*) organized at the village level and have their own songs and chants. Villages fight together in the event of warfare, and when they go to live at dry season cattle camps (*wec*), they often herd their livestock in common (Evans-Pritchard 1951).

TRANSFORMATIONS IN MINNESOTA

Nuer villages in Sudan, then, are communities in every sense of the term, linked together by ties of close personal relationship, mutual participation, and mutual support in a wide range of activities, common interests, and common destinies. These links barely carry over to life in the United States. Villages have been split apart, and the Nuer living in Minnesota may come from many different villages. Younger Nuer, who may have spent much of their lives in refugee camps, often do not even have significant memories of living in a traditional Nuer community. Kinship relationships, though certainly present to some extent, are not as widespread as in Sudan and do not have the same diffuse role in tying everyone together. Though there are groups of brothers, cousins, or individuals linked through marriage, every person is not linked to every other through a well-defined kinship relationship, as was found in traditional village life in Sudan. Similarly, physical security and economic livelihood are no longer linked to other community members. It is no longer necessary to fight side by side with other villagers in warfare, and there are no more cows to herd in common. While in Sudan each person's fate was intimately tied with that of the rest of the community, in the United States each person's fate is largely his or her own.

In this context, the extent to which the Nuer seek to reforge community—albeit on very different terms—is largely a matter of choice, rather than something dictated by the necessities of everyday life. At the same time, the desire to be with other Nuer is prominent. While traditional notions of community have been shattered, language, culture, and shared experiences are a strong pull to bring the Nuer together.

One effect of the desire to create a community is that many distinctions which serve to separate kinsfolk from *rul* (strangers) in Sudan have become less important. In discussing the tribal, clan, and subclan make-up of the Nuer community in Minnesota, one man, for instance, dismissed my questions saying, "Those things don't matter here. Here we are just all Nuer." While this statement may not be entirely true—clan affiliation is the basis for the incipient organization of multistate Nuer associations—it shows the emphasis on qualities they share, rather than on characteristics that divide them.

Two venues have played important roles in serving as new bases for community among the Nuer in Minnesota. Churches have been among the most successful, with several congregations making an effort to provide a place for Nuer Christians to worship, as well as offering a variety of forms of aid. Churches have assumed some importance as centers of Nuer life in Minnesota. I discuss churches in more detail in Chapter 6, when I look at relations between the Nuer and Americans.

The other, less successful venue for community creation has been mutual assistance associations. One mutual assistant association was organized soon after the Nuer became

The Nuer in Minnesota grew up in a Sudanese rural background, as in the scene pictured here.

established in Minnesota while discontented community members have since established others to counter it.

MUTUAL ASSISTANCE ASSOCIATIONS

Throughout the world, mutual assistance associations are common institutions which help immigrants adjust to life in new environments. Whether migrants are simply moving from rural areas to urban areas in search of jobs, or, like the Nuer, across vast distances and international boundaries, the assistance of members of the same ethnic group or people from the same home area can be crucial in making migration a success. Mutual assistance associations are formal organizations through which co-ethnics provide one another with aid in a variety of different ways.

A mutual assistance association was established soon after the Nuer arrived in Minnesota. Ideally this would have served as a locus for community life, while providing information and services crucial to the adjustment of refugees in Minnesota. Unfortunately, this organization instead became a center for community controversy, with a wide range of unresolved accusations against its leadership. A closer look at this conflict brings out some of the difficulties the Nuer face in becoming a community in a new land.

In late 1995, an enterprising young Nuer man, Tut, established a "Sudanese" mutual assistance association. Working in coordination with a well-established Ethiopian mutual assistance association, Tut was given substantial funding by the state of Minnesota to establish an organization for assisting the adjustment of Sudanese refugees in Minnesota. This money was allocated to pay salaries for Tut and an assistant, Buol, as well as for rent and other expenses of setting up a small office in a local church. The principal work of Tut and Buol was to aid in job placement for Sudanese refugees, working in conjunction with social services and church groups. The association was also meant to serve as a center for local Nuer life, as well as a formal voice for the community.

While there was initially a great deal of optimism—particularly among American social service providers who hoped the group would serve as a bridge between the Nuer and the American community—problems soon arose. Who would the organization serve? The group was established as a "Sudanese" organization, yet both its staff and the people whom it served were all Nuer. There were, in fact, other Sudanese—and particularly other southern Sudanese—in the Twin Cities, though living in different parts of the metropolitan area. These included other rural Sudanese, such as members of the Annuak tribe, as well as southern Sudanese from the Equatoria region, who were generally educated, spoke English, and came from a more urban background. Would these Sudanese refugees be included in the leadership of the organization, and what kind services would *they* receive?

This issue quickly became a matter of concern to the Nuer, to other Sudanese in the Twin Cities, as well as to Americans providing the funding for, and assistance to, the organization. At a meeting the organization held to discuss how different constituencies might be brought together, tempers flared between the Nuer and other southern Sudanese, and the meeting nearly ended in violence. Later, as factions developed among the Nuer for control of the organization, accusations of tribal favoritism against opposing sides were used to lobby Americans as well as the Ethiopians overseeing the group.

More problems developed within the organization when, after only a few months, Tut decided he wanted to fire Buol. The reasons for this decision were never clear, but it caused substantial conflict among the Nuer and substantial concern among the Americans. Buol had a reputation for being extremely friendly and helpful, and there was no indication that anyone besides Tut wanted him to go. With the help of the Americans, Buol successfully appealed to the Ethiopian mutual assistance organization—of which the Sudanese organization was a part until getting its own nonprofit status—and was retained. The problems, however, continued. Violence broke out in the office between Buol and a friend of Tut's in a dispute about a car. Buol claimed that he was attacked and that Tut joined in attacking him while Tut claimed that Buol had instigated a fight. Whatever the cause, the violent incident contributed to a continued deterioration of the organization's reputation in the community.

In late spring of 1996 the organization itself got non-profit status and became independent of the Ethiopian mutual assistance association. An independent board was formed which included both Nuer and Americans as well as one Equatorian. After only a short time, however, problems developed again. Contradicting a previous board vote to retain all current employees, Tut had posted a notice to hire a replacement for Buol. This led to acrimony within the board, particularly between Nuer and American members. The Americans felt that Tut was acting in an arbitrary manner, contrary to the direction of the board; the Nuer members were inclined to support Tut (who had selected them for the board). Buol was fired, and within weeks all of the American members had left the board.

The organization never fully righted itself after these early troubles. Although it successfully retained and augmented its funding for a time, and helped specific Nuer at various times, it was never successful in becoming a center of community life. Buol was only the first of many employees to come and go, and community members persisted in allegations against the group. An alternative mutual assistance association was formed—this time with the board elected at a community meeting—but without funding it had trouble functioning as an effective organization.

The kinds of conflicts which plagued the mutual assistance organization are not unusual in the experience of new immigrant groups. Other immigrants in Minnesota, such as the Hmong and Somalis, have undergone similar experiences, as have Nuer communities elsewhere in the United States. (Farnham n.d.) Beyond this common tendency, however, many of the problems experienced by the organization, in failing to form a basis for Nuer community, were rooted in the very process of its creation. The organization did not arise out of the grassroots efforts of the Nuer to come together and organize themselves, but through the awarding of a substantial grant to a small circle of individuals on behalf of the community. Rather than becoming a context through which the Nuer, facing similar problems in a new country, could help one another, leadership of the organization became a prize to be fought over, bringing with it power, prestige, and a high-paying job. Even as the well-intentioned Nuer sought to create alternative organizations, the process through which the original group was formed continued to form their model for a mutual assistance organization. To the Nuer, a community organization was something which had an office and grants, and was not something which emerged simply out of efforts to organize to help one another.

Interestingly, preliminary efforts to form regional mutual assistance associations based on more traditional patterns of organization have been more successful. Members of the Nuer Gaajak clan from Minnesota, Iowa, and Nebraska have formed a group more along ideal models of a mutual assistance organization in which community members come together to help one another in the United States. After this organization's founding, members decided to include other Nuer from the area of Sudan—Maiwut—from which the Gaajak came. This group has held regular meetings in Iowa, and has tried to delineate clear goals for maintaining important aspects of Nuer culture within the refugee community. Members have contributed significant funds, with the idea that these will be used in common projects, such as organizing and providing transportation to community cultural events.

Resettling in Minnesota necessitated many adjustments for the Nuer, some simple, some more complex. The Nuer have had to adjust to new material conditions—living in an apartment, using a stove, and buying food in a store instead of raising it themselves. Perhaps even more importantly, the Nuer have needed to reassess their relationships to one another, to reforge the bases and the nature of community among them. In this sense, the "birth of a community" is not something confined to the early years of resettlement, but is an ongoing process that will continue into the future.

4

Jobs, Welfare, College, and Cars

Shortly after arriving in a Midwestern state, Kun Buol got his first job, working the second shift at a Burger King. Getting to work required taking two separate buses and a 30-minute walk from the second bus to the Burger King. This posed a considerable hardship in the winter months, and there was the ever-present risk that he might be stranded if he got off a bit late since the last bus left shortly after work. Because of these problems, Kun decided to buy a car. However, since he did not have a license he bought the car in his brother's name. While the dealer offered him the car for $1,500 cash, he found it necessary to buy the car through financing and accepted a package totaling over $4,000. He continued making payments even after moving to Minnesota, until one day the car was repossessed. Since the financing agreement stated that the car could not leave the state in which it was purchased, the dealer insisted that the car had to be paid for in full, or else returned to him. Kun was unable to pay in full and he lost the car.

Adjustment to life in Minnesota has not been easy for many of the Nuer, who have faced a constellation of obstacles unusual in their depth and scope even for immigrants. Most Nuer arrived without basic literacy skills, or competence in English, while at the same time having little or no experience with employment or entrepreneurship. And, of course, there are vast differences in the lifestyles and values of Minnesota and Sudan. It is a dramatic shift from a life of subsistence agropastoralism, in which money is not essential and a man of substance is one with many cows, to the United States where daily survival is dependent on working to gain the cash necessary for survival. Indeed, social service workers in Minnesota single out the Nuer as having by far the greatest difficulties in adjusting to life in the United States of any of the other refugees who have settled in Minnesota over the past few decades—Vietnamese, Hmong, and Russian Jews, to name a few of the most prominent.

It is also important to understand the ways in which the Nuer refugees have fit within the particular contours of contemporary American society. As refugees who have fled their homes and lived in camps in Africa, they share problems and concerns with refugees in America from other countries and cultures. Because the Nuer are dependent on welfare or belong to the class of the working poor, they also face problems in Minnesota that confront poor and working-poor, native-born Americans, influenced, as they are, by the particular experiences, cultural understandings, and unique problems that stem from their background as refugees from rural Africa.

LIFESTYLE

In entering Nuer homes, one cannot help but be struck by how little they conform to the images which many Americans have of the "exotic" lifestyles of tribal Africans. Most Nuer live in low-cost apartments of perhaps a 1970s vintage, with aging wall-to-wall carpet, a rather standard layout, and two to three bedrooms. Although few of these apartments are in truly bad condition, most are not well maintained by their landlords: Cracked plaster and leaky toilets are common. Furnishings are also basic. The living room in a typical Nuer apartment is organized around a 25-inch television set, perched atop a sagging particle board entertainment center. A number of secondhand sofas and overstuffed chairs fill the rooms to capacity—daily visits from

Nuer friends create the need for more seating than one might find in a comparable American home. There are few physical clues to the cultural background of the residents, beyond perhaps a thermostat set up to Sahelian standards and the rich aromas of African food wafting from the kitchenette.

It is not, in fact, surprising that there is so little physical evidence of Nuer culture in their homes. Even in Sudan, the Nuer do not have a markedly rich material culture. Clothing of any sort, for instance, has only become common in recent decades, and they have no indigenous textile tradition of the sort found in other parts of Africa. Also, there are few well-developed forms of visual art, such as mask making or other types of woodcarving. The few material items in a traditional Nuer household are spears and other weapons, cooking utensils and household implements, and personal effects such as beads, other ornaments, and smoking pipes. The Nuer have brought few of these items with them. As refugees from Africa who traveled hundreds of miles—sometimes more than a thousand miles—on foot and overcrowded public transport, it was extremely difficult to carry personal belongings, including

Suburban apartments are the most common living situation for the Nuer, with ample seating provided for frequent guests.

any distinctively Nuer cultural items they might have owned. Typically, a few strings of black and white beads are the only items of Nuer material culture in a refugee home. In Minnesota, the Nuer eat a range of both American and African foods. African foods include Nuer foods and those which entered their cuisine during their stay in refugee camps in Ethiopia. A mainstay of the diet is *njerra*, a spongy bread which is a staple food in Ethiopia and is eaten with meat or vegetable stews. *Koff*, a Nuer food made with cornmeal and meat or fish, is also commonly eaten. Some American foods—particularly prepared foods, such as frozen pizza—are increasingly part of the Nuer diet. Most Nuer do not like canned and other processed foods, however. Even milk, which is a major dietary component in Sudan and considered by Nuer to be the most perfect, most complete food, is disdained by many Nuer in the United States, who find the taste of American milk to be different from their own milk, and markedly unappealing.

Daily schedules are largely governed by the necessities of life in the United States rather than by the cultural frameworks for time which the Nuer brought with them to this country. In Sudan, as in much of Africa and other rural areas around the world, time is structured in flexible ways, governed not by rigid schedules but by the time requirements of particular tasks—the care of livestock, the cultivation of land, and the need to hold meetings to discuss community issues. Evans-Pritchard, in his study of the Nuer in the 1930s, made much of the way that Nuer time was reckoned in relation to significant social events, rather than as an abstract entity which moved along apart from the activities of human beings. Seasons were reckoned by the activities which took place—cultivation, moving to cattle camps, or returning from them to the villages (Evans-Pritchard 1951). The passage of time might be understood in relation to a ceremony, or a wedding, or in counting the number of "sleeps" since a particular event. A time of day might be described as "at milking" or "when the sun was warming up." Viewed from the standpoint of a European whose life was dictated by a clock and a calendar, he speaks admiringly of the easy way in which the Nuer view time:

> . . . the Nuer have no expression equivalent to "time" in our language, and cannot, therefore . . . speak of time as though it were something actual which passes, can be wasted, can be saved and so forth. I do not think that they ever experience the same feeling of fighting against time or having to co-ordinate activities with an abstract passage of time, because their points of reference are mainly the activities themselves, which are generally of a leisurely character. Events follow a logical order, but they are not controlled by an abstract system, there being no autonomous points of reference to which activities have to conform with precision. Nuer are fortunate (1951: 103).

The Nuer in Minnesota are not so "fortunate." In the United States, the Nuer have found that being on time matters. Appointments may be cancelled if one fails to arrive on time, tardiness at work may lead to dismissal, and classes begin whether students have arrived or not. As refugees who typically enter the work force at its lowest rungs, their schedules can be all the more difficult. Working nights or other odd hours is commonplace, as the Nuer take jobs which most Americans do not want. While this transition has not been easy, the Nuer have nevertheless come to accept the fact that their daily schedules in the United States are governed largely by the economic necessities of their lives.

ECONOMIC LIFE

The Nuer face radical differences between the economic life they are familiar with in Sudan and the economic environment of the United States. The Nuer come from a rural, and rather remote, area of Sudan. In Sudan, their economic life is based on subsistence agropastoralism, characterized by the cultivation of maize and millet using hand tools and household labor, and the raising of livestock, including cattle, sheep, and goats. While many Nuer sell crops, and particularly livestock, with some regularity, production is primarily oriented towards household use. Families build their own houses out of grass, sticks, and other locally available materials. Cash needs are highly limited, and generally directed towards items whose purchase is nonessential or which can be delayed without extreme hardship, for instance, new or fancy clothing. In any case, one's livelihood is rarely dependent on access to cash on a daily basis.

This is obviously not the case in Minnesota—and the Nuer are well aware of the contrast. While most Nuer speak of life in the United States in positive terms, the constant need for money is vexing. One man spoke of the excitement of receiving $250 on arrival in the United States, only to be faced with the disillusionment of discovering how little this seemingly handsome sum bought in America. The Nuer commonly speak of the advantages of life in Africa in such terms as "It is very cheap to live there" and "There is nothing like rent there." The Nuer enjoy the material advantages of life in the United States, but find that at times the costs can be difficult to bear.

Similarly, the need for employment and the work conditions in the United States were foreign to the Nuer upon arrival. In Sudan, many men had some type of wage work experience, but both the conditions and goals differed radically from what they found in this country. Many young Nuer men, such as Gatluak Luoth (now in his thirties), went to cities to engage in migratory wage labor while still in Sudan. In the 1980s, Gatluak made frequent trips to Khartoum to work as a day laborer in the construction industry. At other times of the year he traveled from Khartoum to do seasonal agricultural work elsewhere in Sudan. Unlike in the United States, there was no need to fill out an application; you showed up, and if help was needed, you worked.

To seek work away from his home community was a choice Gatluak made—an attractive and sensible option at a stage in his life when he was unmarried, had limited responsibilities at home, and was attracted to the opportunity to earn money for both the frivolities of youth and to prepare economically for married life. Returning from months of work, he had independent access to cash which allowed him to purchase livestock, clothing for himself and his family, and fancy dance regalia. As Hutchinson (1996) notes, these items were particularly important in establishing a young man's prestige, and allowed him to be successful in courting girls in his home area. A famous girl's saying went: "If he comes back from the north, and his dog recognizes him, don't converse with him!" (Hutchinson 1996: 26).

An essential goal of young men traveling to Khartoum for wage labor, then, was to acquire fancy clothes, colorful leggings, sunglasses and the like, which would make them attractive to Nuer girls, to transform them into somebody glamorous and important. Work was not essential to their livelihood, and it was something that they could—and did—abandon as they desired to do so. Indeed, assuming the responsibilities of family life would force young men to abandon their life of migrating to Khartoum for work (Hutchinson 1996: p. 175). In the United States, in contrast, work is driven by the necessity of everyday survival, in order to support oneself or a family. Day after day must be spent at low-paying, unattractive jobs in order to buy food and clothing and pay the rent and other bills.

Buol Tang's hectic pace working in the United States is in stark contrast to the more leisurely rhythms of the life he knew in Sudan. Rather than spending his days cultivating the fields, herding livestock, and visiting and discussing shared concerns with other village men, Buol works nights as a security guard. During the day, he is sleeping or in school, where he hopes to gain skills to attain a better paying job. The stress of this way of life not only falls on Buol but on his family as well. His wife Nyabuom says that one reason she would like to return to Sudan is that here people are always working. The stress of having to follow a rigid work schedule in order to make ends meet and get ahead here can be overwhelming—particularly when a car breaks down or a child gets sick. In Buol's case, for instance, repeated automobile problems forced him to abandon his job as a security guard.

Nuer men are typically hardworking and interested in finding jobs. To new arrivals, however, the discipline of the American workplace is unusual and many have difficulties adjusting to it. American employers' expectation that workers will arrive on time and every day is in stark contrast to the rhythms of rural life in Sudan and even to conditions of migratory wage work in which some Nuer men had engaged.

Rural life does not run on a time clock, nor does wage work necessarily take priority over events—such as the sickness of a child—which might arise unexpectedly. The Nuer have generally been able to adjust to differences in work expectations between Sudan and the United States, but problems in gaining and holding employment persist. Most notably, language barriers and lack of education, job experience, and job skills make it difficult to find a job that pays a living wage. Some Nuer have sought to improve their employment prospects through additional education. English as a Second Language (ESL) classes have been popular among women, but less so among men. Since Nuer men often knew more English than women when they arrived in the United States, classes are generally not tailored to their needs. Many Nuer men have been reticent to participate in classes filled predominantly with Nuer women, and which they see as something for women.

A number of younger Nuer men have decided to continue to pursue their education by attending community college. Many had attended secondary school in Ethiopia, and were particularly attracted to the opportunity to come to America by the promise of further study. Most of these men are past high school age, but do not have the academic and language skills to attend a four-year college. They also do not have transcripts or diplomas to prove their educational background. Community colleges offer open admissions which allow the Nuer to attend despite these problems.

Courses of study typically fall into two main categories. Many take some kind of basic English classes to improve their language and writing skills. Along with this, some opt for a very general course of study, without any particular goal, but with the idea that education will help them get ahead in the United States and move them beyond low-wage, menial work. Others take courses at community schools or technical colleges which they hope will train them for particular types of work—for instance, the nursing assistant training programs.

In some cases, the Nuer have been able to gain some degree of economic independence, through further education, hard work, or good luck. For many, however, gaining the skills and opportunities for economic success remains a hope for the future. As a result, most Nuer—and in particular those living in families—have remained, to varying degrees, dependent on public assistance.

MAKING A LIVING

The economic environment of the Twin Cities in the mid-1990s made it relatively easy for the Nuer to find jobs of some kind. Minnesota's diversified economy has traditionally offered some protection against recessions, and the economic vitality of the mid-1990s created a high demand for labor. In September 1996, for instance, the unemployment rate in Minnesota was only 3.2 percent. The relative ease with which most Nuer have been able to find jobs is, however, in stark contrast to their difficulties in keeping jobs, supporting a family on wages they earn, and continuing to be able to take care of family responsibilities, particularly the care of children.

The work available to most Nuer is generally in low-paying, and often undesirable, jobs. In other parts of the midwest, the Nuer have found the meat packing industry to be an important source of relatively good-paying jobs— $8.00–$9.00 per hour. The downside is that meat packing is dirty, difficult, and dangerous even if it pays well in comparison to other unskilled and low-skill labor. Indeed, one Nuer man moved to Minneapolis after having lost a finger in an accident at a meat packing plant in another state. Whatever the advantages and disadvantages of meat packing, however, jobs in this industry are not readily available in the Twin Cities. Instead, the Nuer have found work in light industry, as janitors, as security guards, and in the fast-food industry. These jobs require little training, as well as minimal language skills. Some Nuer with greater English ability have taken courses and acquired the qualifications to become nursing assistants, a job which is in high demand but does not require a great deal of training.

The difficulties of finding and holding a job which pays a living wage have made welfare a major component of Nuer economic adjustment to life in Minnesota. While Nuer families have gained greater economic independence as they have lived longer in the United States, all of the Nuer in

Minnesota have been on public assistance at some point, and most continue to qualify for at least partial benefits. In the earliest stages of resettlement, the Nuer have had some small advantages within the welfare system, because they were eligible as refugees for specific entitlements designed to aid in their adjustment to a new country. After three months, however, they are placed within the same general welfare system serving native-born Americans. Unlike other legal immigrants whom recent legislation has excluded from welfare, refugees continue to be eligible for five years.

Recent reforms of the welfare system will have a significant impact on the Nuer. There are now lifetime limits on the receipt of benefits (sixty months). To receive benefits one must either work or be involved in job search activities on a nearly full-time basis. This requirement was broadened in 1998 to require both parents to spend significant numbers of hours in work/job-seeking activities in order to maintain eligibility for welfare.

A variety of factors make choices concerning welfare and work difficult ones for the Nuer. Welfare recipients may retain a portion of their benefits even while working until they have reached a certain income level, but the extra money earned in a job is offset by the rigid schedules and long hours of often mind-numbing work. When Buol Tang decided to add full-time work to full-time school, he ended up with only about $300 more a month than he had been receiving through welfare alone, despite the enormous strains it put on his life (see ACHSC n.d.). Despite sound long-term reasons, then, for entering the work force, such as gaining job experience and a work record to aid in future employment, some Nuer prefer to collect welfare, even if they can do so only for five years.

Some Nuer who work do not always report their earnings to the county social services department, as is required. Since their earnings would reduce the benefits for which they are eligible, it is considered welfare fraud not to report them. If caught committing welfare fraud, their families face a potential penalty of losing all benefits for three months. The chances of getting caught eventually are almost certain because social services can verify reported income through quarterly tax information filed by employers.

The loss of welfare benefits can be sudden and cause extreme stress for a family. Ganwar Tual was one of the leaders of the secondary migration of Nuer refugees to Minnesota, having been one of the first to move there from another state. At around age forty he was one of the older members of the community, and was highly regarded among the Nuer for his generosity and respectful manner—skills which he had put to good use in Sudan where he had been a village chief. In Minnesota, however, he had gained a reputation at social services not only as being prone to welfare fraud himself, but as someone who also encouraged others to commit it. In fact, it was suspected that he had encouraged other Nuer to come to Minnesota by telling them that enforcement was lax and that they could work without reporting income and still collect welfare benefits. Since coming to Minnesota he had moved several times, and his welfare case worker suspected that he did so because cases weren't tracked well between counties.

In late 1995, while living in the northern metropolitan area, he lost a full-time job. Ganwar claimed that he had been attacked and thrown into a dumpster by coworkers, and that he had suffered injuries that affected his ability to work. He felt that he was entitled to time off and that his inability to work was directly related to his injuries. In contrast, his employer asserted that the "attack" was not as severe as Ganwar claimed, and that Ganwar had left the job voluntarily by failing to report to work for a variety of spurious (in the employer's estimation) reasons which were unrelated to the incident. The county ruled that he had left work voluntarily and therefore denied him benefits. Ganwar lost all assistance and was told that he would need to wait for three months before reapplying. His family of six was left without any source of income and were unable to pay their rent. Shortly thereafter they left the Twin Cities for a small town elsewhere in Minnesota.

Public assistance is an important factor in decisions the Nuer make concerning their living situations—if they should work, how much they should work, and where they should live. The Nuer are particularly interested in any opportunities to lower their housing costs, since the vast majority of their income goes to paying rent. A major reason that many

Nuer left Minnesota for Nebraska in 1997 was because of the availability of subsidized housing there. Subsequently, the Nuer became aware of a program through which they could get subsidized housing in the Twin Cities if they lived for a period of time in a rural area of Minnesota. A number of families moved to a small town not far from the Twin Cities, with the hope of returning to cheap housing in a year's time.

Another problem which the Nuer face in making a living in Minnesota is affordable child care. Because it is not possible to adequately support a family on a $6.00/hour job, the Nuer recognize that a husband and wife must both work if they are going to make ends meet. The Nuer are generally comfortable with other people looking after their children because in the village setting in Sudan there is a great deal of sharing responsibility for children. Children wander between homes in the village, and other adults frequently keep an eye on children while their parents are busy elsewhere. These same mechanisms for sharing child care are not present among the Nuer in Minnesota. In Sudan, grandparents are frequently enlisted to look after children, but there are no grandparents in Minnesota. Further, since a lack of affordable housing has served to disperse Nuer families, it is difficult to make regular arrangements for sharing child care. The Nuer generally find child care to be an acceptable option but face serious obstacles in its affordability and availability. Because child-care costs frequently exceed $5.00/hour per child, it simply does not make sense to work at a job that may not even pay for the child care. While government funds are increasingly available for child-care assistance, it can be difficult to qualify. In addition, the rules may be difficult to understand and negotiate (particularly for refugees), and it can be hard to find licensed child-care providers even if a family receives assistance.

In seeking economic independence, a final barrier is often transportation. In order to work, one must be able to get to where the job is. In this sense, the Nuer's class position in the United States is salient in shaping their life experiences here. As it is for native-born Americans, the location of workplaces in contemporary American cities can be a significant barrier to getting to work. A variety of factors have increasingly shifted employment sites from city centers to suburban areas (Gordon, Richardson and Yu 1998; Harris 1997), a process that has taken place in the Twin Cities as well. As elsewhere, public transportation is well suited to bringing people from suburbs to city and back again, but moving from suburb to suburb is difficult and time consuming; it is frequently necessary to travel into the city and back out again simply to reach an adjacent suburb. This poses particular problems for immigrants such as the Nuer (Preston, McLafferty and Liu 1998). For workers on the late or evening shifts—like many Nuer—public transportation is often completely unavailable. Jobs may be relatively easy to find, but it may be difficult to keep them, and the effort to get to work may simply not be worth it.

In response, most Nuer have purchased automobiles. Buying a car enables them to work; it is also a way that the Nuer enthusiastically pursue the acquisition of an "American lifestyle." Yet although cars help the Nuer, they bring many difficulties as well.

A CAR IS A BAD COW

"So what did your friends tell you about life in the United States?" I asked Buom in an interview focusing on images of the United States that the Nuer had before coming here. He had told me that when he was in a refugee camp in Kenya he had had telephone conversations with friends who had already resettled here.

Affecting an African-American accent, Buom replied in English, "'You can get a good job, get a car, man!" and he laughed.

The automobile has come to have a special significance for the Nuer in Minnesota and has played a central role in shaping their lives, in some sense similar to the way their cows did in Sudan. Indeed, the Nuer joke that "In Africa we have cows; here we have cars." Although spoken in jest, this statement shows the strong and conscious engagement of Nuer with American culture, which, as they have correctly assessed, is deeply focused on the automobile. Just as Nuer culture in Sudan is centered on cows as densely packed material and symbolic objects around which their economic, social, and ritual life is woven, American's depend on automobiles for their economic well-being, as well as to define their social identity. In making the connection between cars and cows, the Nuer are keen observers of the concrete and metaphorical relationship between these items in Nuer and American culture. At the same time, equating cows and cars is an ironic—though good-natured—commentary on the ways their lives have changed from savannah herders to suburban commuters. Their economic livelihood and their personal prestige are now tied up in something with four wheels and one horn, rather than four legs and two horns.

Yet, as one man joked, "A car is a bad cow." A cow seldom gives you problems unless it is sick and about to die. In contrast, a car constantly gives you problems. Particularly in a place like Minnesota, with its extreme winter climate, cars frequently break down. This is exacerbated by the fact that few of the Nuer can afford a car that is in good condition. They frequently purchase cars from unscrupulous dealers who take advantage of the Nuer's lack of experience and inability to assess the condition and value of a car. The result is that mechanical problems are common. There are other problems, too. Since the Minnesota driver's license examination has not been translated into the Nuer language, passing the test can be a trial, and individuals sometimes choose to drive without a license. Proper insurance is costly, and legal problems may arise if the Nuer fail to get insurance. Many Nuer buy cars in order to get to work only to find they are working just to maintain a car—making monthly car payments along with the expenses of insurance and repairs. The income earned to pay for the car may also affect welfare benefits. Consequently, cars can have a tremendous impact on restructuring family life.

The case of Buol Tang offers a vivid example. In the spring of 1996 he bought a used minivan. At the time he was employed at an unusually well-paying job and had no difficulties with the expenses of the car, including a monthly car payment of $300. Although he could get to work without a car, he had a large family and wanted to use the car to go shopping and to visit other Nuer who lived farther away.

Unfortunately, a few months later he was fired from his job, and shortly thereafter he decided that it would be a good idea to get additional education and training at a local community college. He continued, however, to feel the necessity of paying for the van, which neither he nor his wife wished to lose. For a few months he was able to scrape together enough money to make his monthly payments but soon found it impossible through public assistance alone. Rather than risk repossession, he sought new employment. While the amount of income above welfare which he earned was quite small—only a few hundred dollars a month—he hoped it would be enough to meet his car expenses.

Unfortunately, other consequences resulted from this strategy. He spent so much time working that it was difficult to continue with his studies, and he ended up reducing his course load. Meanwhile, his income rose to a level at which his eligibility for general cash assistance from the county—which he depended on to pay the rent—was cut off. Now forced to work more hours to pay the rent, he found it impossible to continue with school. Finally he was unable to meet all of his automobile expenses, particularly after a series of costly repairs stemming from the car's poor mechanical condition. Unable to pay all of his bills, he chose to pay his car payment (rather than risk repossession) instead of his car insurance. Shortly thereafter his cousin had an accident while driving the car. Buol was unable to pay for the repairs, decided not to continue the car payments, and the van was repossessed. Despite having lost the car—which had been his primary impetus to leave school for work—he had problems leaving his job because a person cannot collect welfare benefits if he or she has willingly left a job.

Buol's case is striking in the way that one event after another restructured his life, with a car at the root of his troubles. In other cases, car-related problems are sudden and disastrous, rather than chronic over a long period of time. Weu Both is a young man in his early twenties who was imprisoned in early 1997 after having been convicted of attempted robbery for trying to hold up a woman in a convenience store parking lot. The impetus for his crime was believed by community members to be an auto accident.

Driving his cousin's car without a license or insurance, he damaged the building at his place of work. When a judge ruled that he was liable for $12,000 in damages, he is reputed to have gone crazy and attempted robbery in order to get money. In nearby Iowa a similar, but even more horrible, incident occurred when a Nuer man, faced with thousands of dollars in fines for repeated offenses of driving without a license and drunken driving, disappeared. His body was found a week later; he had gone to a nearby woods and hanged himself.

These are not isolated cases, as shown by quantitative data collected from a sample of 19 Nuer men in early 1998. All reported having owned one or more cars in the United States, and most of them (84%) owned a car at the time of the survey. All had driven for at least two years, and none had driven more than five, with the average length of driving experience being 3.15 years. Virtually all had experienced a serious problem in the short time that they had driven. A majority had been in an automobile accident (64%); an equal number (64%) had lost at least one car in unfavorable circumstances. In just over three years that the average Nuer had been driving, 84 percent had had an accident, had a car repossessed or impounded, or been forced to abandon a car because of irreparable mechanical problems! The Nuer go through cars at an amazing rate—48 cars in a total of 60 driving years, and almost half of all cars purchased (48%) were lost under unfavorable circumstances. Very few, then, have found car ownership to be a process devoid of serious mishap.

There are notable differences in many aspects of Nuer car ownership and use in comparison with the American population. Americans, for instance, typically treat the acquisition of a learner's permit and driver's license as the first steps in becoming a driver. In contrast, most Nuer (79%) reported having purchased and driven their first car prior to obtaining a license. Often this is due to difficulties in passing the driver's license exam, the written portion in particular. Almost all (90%) took the written test more than once, and the average Nuer retook it more than three times. One result—beyond the obvious danger of being on the road as an untrained driver—is that difficulties with the law or insurance companies frequently result from driving without a license.

Beyond passing the driving test, there is a clear need for more driving training, as the high auto accident rates show. Indeed, more than a quarter (26%) had totaled one or more cars. While within the general population there is an accident rate of 8.3 incidents per hundred driving years (HLDI: 1993), the Nuer drivers I surveyed had a rate more than three and a half times that, at 30 accidents per hundred driving years.

Along with the problems caused by accidents, the Nuer spend a phenomenal amount of money on their cars. The total cost for all cars (that Nuer reported having bought) averaged $10,363 per respondent! The amount that they had actually spent was much lower—because so many cars were lost before they were fully paid for—but cash purchases and down payments still averaged $1,245 per driver, per year. Amazingly, despite the fact that most Nuer have been on public assistance, they have had easy access to car loans. Almost half of the cars (46%) were bought on loan, with monthly payments on these loans averaging $195 a month. Not surprisingly, the Nuer defaulted on quite a high percentage of these loans (37%) and had their cars repossessed. Clearly, Nuer refugees are subject to exploitation by unscrupulous creditors of the type found in the classified section of all major newspapers: "No Credit? Bad Credit? We'll Finance You." Typically such dealers require a down payment equal to their costs, charge high rates of interest, and repossess and sell the car again if payments are not met (Thomas n.d.). Kun Buol's experiences, discussed at the beginning of this chapter, illustrate these problems well. Because he got a loan from a dealer, he needed to pay more than twice the value of the car. When he was unable to pay in full on moving to Minnesota, the car was repossessed.

Car repairs can also pose serious problems for Nuer drivers. Frequently the cars they purchase are not in good condition; 17 percent of the cars purchased were abandoned because of mechanical failure. The Nuer often do not have enough knowledge of automobiles to ensure that they are treated fairly by mechanics. The difficulties that the Nuer have with mechanics is illustrated in the experience of Buol, who had his car towed to a mechanic when it wouldn't start. He was first told that the car needed a new battery, but after replacing the battery, the car broke down again. He was then told that the alternator was bad—which was, of course, the reason why the battery had gone dead before. Then the mechanic insisted that the battery in the car was not the one he had put in a week previously—this, he claimed, was a cheap Walmart battery—and he insisted on replacing it for $60. Eventually Buol lost his job. He couldn't get to work without his car, and the mechanic refused to release his car until he paid the $500 repair bill. In response to this chain of events, Buol noted ironically: "Mechanics are like the magicians we have in Africa. It doesn't matter if what they say is true—you have to pay them anyway."

Implicit in this discussion is the question of why Nuer refugees have such an intense interest in automobiles, so that the acquisition and maintenance can have such an overriding influence on all aspects of their lives. Economic necessity is clearly an important factor, and the one most frequently cited by the Nuer themselves, but it is not the only one. While studies of both low-income, native-born Americans and immigrants have demonstrated that automobiles can have important effects on income, total automobile expenses for the Nuer average as much as $4,000 a year—far exceeding any possible economic gains from automobile ownership.

Clearly other factors are at play. It is interesting to note that in all cases, informants reported having purchased their first car through work earnings; that is, they were already working prior to buying the vehicle. While vehicle ownership may have broadened their opportunities and made work more accessible, it was not actually a necessity. Temporary agencies sometimes provided transportation to job sites, and rides were sometimes available from friends. The experiences of welfare workers also suggest that the Nuer's interest in cars goes beyond simple material considerations. A common report from welfare offices is that the Nuer encounter problems with eligibility for welfare benefits because they voluntarily leave jobs after having purchased a car. The Nuer maintained in these cases that they were not really working, but rather were only temporarily employed for the purposes of purchasing a car—an interpretation to which County Human Services were not generally sympathetic.

Cars bring social benefits, allowing the Nuer to shop more easily and visit friends. In fact, the Nuer who do not themselves have cars, generally have to ask friends for rides, and this has real or potential social costs. The Nuer speak of "annoying people," of putting a burden upon them with too frequent requests. Here, indigenous Nuer attitudes towards patron/client relationships may enter in, as well. Hutchinson (1996) notes that a community leader is someone who shares freely, while restricting his reliance on the hospitality of others. In America, having to ask for assistance with rides too frequently may be tied up in personal prestige. Stated simply, a person with a car is a patron, one without a car is a client.

A car, in addition, is in itself an important symbol of prestige. Even prior to resettlement, in refugee camps half a world a way, the Nuer were already thinking about and talking about cars. Cars formed a central image for the wealth that they hoped to attain in America. As one man noted, "In Africa if you have no money in your pocket but you have a car, you are a rich man." In acquiring an automobile, the Nuer attain at least the symbols of a class position that most of them could not have hoped to have held in Africa.

And this brings us back to the analogy to cows with which I began. If cows are something that the Nuer love and around which their lives are organized, quite similar things may be said of the car in American culture—a fact not lost on the Nuer. As the Nuer adapt to American life, it is not surprising that the automobile is embraced as a central part of that transformation.

CONCLUSION

Adjustment to life in Minnesota has presented many challenges for the Nuer, as they struggle to find ways to make ends meet in a radically new environment. Where once they herded cattle and tilled the soil, they now work in low-end jobs in an industrial economy, exposed to the pressures of the time clock and working to pay for their cars. Balancing options available to them in the form of employment and welfare presents difficult decisions, as they also try to parent their children and acquire skills which will provide them with a better life in the future. Issues of economic well-being not only are central to Nuer life in Minnesota in the present, but need perhaps most importantly to be addressed in regard to the long-term well-being of the Nuer community.

5

Gender, Generation, and Family Change

The spread of food filled the living room as grocery bags were emptied indiscriminately. With their car broken down, shopping had been impossible for several days, and the family was hungry—not only Buol, Nyabuom, and their children, but also a distantly related woman and her teenage children who had recently arrived from Ethiopia and were temporarily staying at their home. When I showed up at their apartment, Buol and Nyabuom asked if I could take them shopping, and we went together to the nearest Cub Foods. There they filled two carts with a vast array of foods. When we returned home, children and adults alike sifted through the bags hungrily, grabbing fruit, precooked chicken wings, and macaroni and jello salads of various kinds. Buol went over to the VCR and popped in a tape which, he explained, his two-year-old daughter really enjoyed—"Barney's Great Adventure." As it played practically everyone joined in singing happy songs with the big, purple dinosaur.

This family scene is in many ways typical of both continuity and change from Nuer life in Sudan to Nuer life in Minnesota. While much of the context is radically different— jello salad and Barney, rather than milk or porridge with cows lowing in the background—the style of personal interaction is in many ways similar. In a sense this was a family meal, yet to an outsider it appeared as chaos, each person finding what they could and eating together but in no apparently organized way. There was no table, no serving of food, and—though in this instance the television became the center of shared attention—no group conversation per se. While the importance of the togetherness of the family was evident, it was expressed very differently than in an American home.

The family continues to be a centerpiece of Nuer life in the United States, as it is in Sudan. Relationships between men and women and young and old center on the family, which is the focus of both social and economic activity. (By family, I mean the nuclear (or in Sudan, polygynous) family, as opposed to the broader kinship network.) Yet new stresses now face Nuer families, and their forms of family life have been transformed in response to new needs and new constraints in Minnesota.

Nowhere is this more evident than in relations between men and women in Nuer marriages. Some of the changes are fairly superficial and are relatively easy to adjust to. That Buol and Nyabuom went together to buy food, for instance, differs markedly from the responsibilities of men and women in Sudan, where food provisioning is central to female roles and defined as wholly outside of male spheres. Other changes in gender roles have caused more problems, and there are new arenas for conflict and fewer ways to resolve family problems. Similarly, youth now face new challenges and experiences that were unknown to rural Africa.

NUER FAMILY LIFE IN SUDAN

A Nuer homestead is spread across an open area, within the general grouping of a village. The homestead's center is a massive mud and grass structure, *luak*, which looks onto a thorn fence enclosure for the family's cattle and is surrounded by smaller huts belonging to the women of the family. The physical layout of the Nuer homestead reflects some of the most important aspects of Nuer family relationships, defining the gender roles and relationships between husbands and wives as well as relationships between parents and their children (Evans-Pritchard 1951). The family (*gol*) is often polygynous, with Nuer men marrying several wives. The polygynous family is the center of Nuer economic life; the herding of cattle and the raising of crops are organized within the domestic group. Each wife has her own house (*dwil*) and her own cooking fire (*mac*) to which she and her children belong (Evans-Pritchard 1951). As such, traditional Nuer families are composed of a number of female-centered families nested within a broader family group. While the Nuer consider it very important to maintain the unity of the family underneath the father, tensions inevitably arise among members of different houses. Jealousy is the norm between co-wives, based not so much in romantic competition for their shared husband but in resources, work responsibilities, and other forms of possible favoritism (Hutchinson 1996). Similarly, the sons of different wives are in a position of competition for the family's cattle, which they will eventually inherit, and need to start families of their own.

Among the most important aspects of traditional Nuer family life is the process of marriage. The Nuer marriage serves to unite two extended families as much as it serves to unite a single couple. A wide kinship network is involved in the process of marrying and continues to have considerable influence over the couple long after the marriage is completed. The most important aspect of the involvement of the kinship network is the payment of bridewealth cattle—usually 25 to 40 animals—from the family of the groom to the family of the bride. These animals are drawn not only from the herd of the groom's father, but from a variety of uncles and cousins within the kinship network. The bridewealth cattle go not only to the bride's nuclear family, but also to many other members of her extended kin group. The main purpose of the bridewealth payment is to transfer membership of the bride from her father's family to the family of the groom, and to make any children resulting from the marriage legitimate members of the groom's family (Evans-Pritchard 1951; Hutchinson 1996).

Despite the important involvements of the kinship network in marriage, Nuer marriages are not typically "arranged" in the sense found in many societies where the groom, and particularly the bride, have little choice in selecting their partners. Sometimes the couple may be friends or lovers before marriage, although real affection is more often something which develops in the course of their long lives together (Duany 1992). The consent of both, however, is considered necessary for the success of the marriage. At the same time, tension and conflict within marriage are considered normal, rather than deviant and harmful. The Nuer characterize the couple as "two people who can't agree on anything" (Hutchinson 1996, p. 229), and marriage is characterized by a jostling of the wills of the two parties.

According to Nuer masculine ideals, the man should be the ruler of the home, and his wife should unquestioningly act according to his will. Nuer women often see things differently. Conflict frequently arises over a variety of different issues, often centering on the care of the home, the treatment of guests, perceived inequalities in the treatment of co-wives, or alleged female adultery. Within these conflicts, male recourse to physical violence is considered normal and is a frequent occurrence. Women, in contrast, often exert considerable influence over their husbands by withholding food or by returning to their families of birth and possibly seeking divorce. Divorce is becoming an increasingly common feature in rural Nuer life. In 1936, Evans-Pritchard estimated that only six percent of Leek Nuer women had ever been divorced, compared to 36 percent found by Hutchinson in 1983 (Hutchinson 1990, 1996). Much of this stems from ongoing changes in Nuer social relationships derived from the imposition of courts and external government rule beginning in the 1930s. The extended kin network, however, continues to exert considerable influence over the marital couple. Kin seek to keep the couple together both for the sake of the marriage and for the messy consequences for both families in the event of divorce, due to the necessity of returning the bridewealth cattle.

Children are raised to respect and obey their parents, with corporal punishment the most common form of discipline. Even into adulthood, it is expected that children will continue to follow the will of their parents (and their father in particular) out of respect and affection, as well as the threat of disinheritance and the fear of parental curses. At the same time, Nuer parents value physical strength and strength of will, and proudly cultivate these attributes in their children. This is illustrated in an incident observed by Hutchinson (1996), in which a young Nuer boy threw a broken brick at his mother in the course of an argument. Rather than becoming angry, the mother said with pride: "Did you see my little boy throw a brick at me?" Far from being angry or disturbed at this show of disrespect, his mother found his strength of will to be admirable.

REFUGEE FLIGHT AND THE NUER FAMILY

The disruption of their life in Sudan, and flight from the civil war in Sudan, brought many changes to the family lives of Nuer refugees. The war itself broke up many families. Some members were killed in fighting or died from disease or starvation; others fled to live with relatives in areas where the fighting was not as intense; others left for refugee camps in Ethiopia; and others took their chances and stayed behind. It was unusual for whole families to reach the camps intact, and rarer still for whole families to eventually reach the United States. Particularly because most of the Nuer in Minnesota are relatively young, only a handful of Nuer were married in Sudan prior to experiencing the chaos of war.

Most of the Nuer who reached the United States came to the refugee camps on their own, or accompanied by siblings or cousins, though some were accompanied by parents. As the opportunity arose to seek asylum in the United States, it was almost exclusively the younger generation who undertook the arduous journey from Ethiopia to Kenya to apply for resettlement.

Most marriages of Nuer in Minnesota were formed somewhere within this process of flight and resettlement— some in camps in Ethiopia, others in Kenya just prior to resettlement, and a few after having resettled in the United States. I was surprised one day to receive an invitation to Buol Tang's wedding, since I knew his wife and his three children quite well. Although they were living as husband

and wife, I learned that they had never actually managed to get officially married. Having met during the disruption caused by the civil war in Ethiopia, their life together was spent moving from place to place, and they never had the resources to wed. More than five years after the fact, they married in a church wedding in Minnesota.

Usually it was difficult for couples to get married while in flight, and a traditional Nuer wedding ceremony was out of the question. In contemporary war-ravaged Sudan, it has been difficult to raise the 25 cows considered the minimum for appropriate Nuer bridewealth, as Nuer herds have been looted to feed both government and rebel forces. Those living in refugee camps generally have no livestock available to them, and they usually live apart from relatives who could provide them with additional livestock. Most of the bride's kin who would normally be involved in marriage are also absent. Sometimes money is substituted for cattle in marriages formed in Ethiopia, Kenya, or the United States, either as a direct payment or (particularly in the case of money remitted from Minnesota) to purchase livestock to be paid as bridewealth. While the use of money as a marriage payment was regarded until recently as inappropriate—because money lacks the social significance of cattle—the Nuer have come to accept it because of the disruption of civil war.

The fact is that the marriages of many couples living in the United States are highly questionable by Nuer standards. Many have not paid bridewealth and have performed neither traditional Nuer or Christian marriage ceremonies. While they are recognized as husband and wife, because they live together and state their intention of completing a marriage ceremony, they are not truly married.

An important change in Nuer marriage brought about by refugee flight is that the married couple has become an isolated social unit, rather than one embedded within a wide kinship network. In part, this relates to the widespread absence of bridewealth; the kinship network was not brought into the process of marriage formation and has little tangible stake in its outcome. More important is the absence of a wider kinship network in Minnesota. While many of the Nuer have a few brothers, sisters, or cousins scattered around

Minnesota or other parts of the United States, there is no cohesive kinship group to play a daily role in assisting a couple in their relationship. Nuer couples are in many ways very much alone in facing the new struggles that they have encountered in Minnesota.

One additional factor to note in examining differences in gender relations among the Nuer in Minnesota and Sudan is that most couples are quite young. In Sudan, it is only when Nuer women move into middle age that they have more equal relationships with their husbands. Few Nuer women in Minnesota have reached that age.

Nuer marriages, in Minnesota as in Sudan, typically involve an age gap between husbands and wives. In Sudan, Nuer women typically marry between the ages of 15 to 17, while their husbands might be in their mid-twenties. While the husband is considered a man, entering into the prime of life, the wife is still considered a girl until she has given birth to a child. Only when her children start to mature does she start to gain power and authority in relation to her husband. This may be attributed to a variety of factors: her own increased maturity and self-confidence; social norms concerning the behavior of older and younger women; and the influence gained by her closer relationship with her children, who are now themselves forging a place in the community. Among older couples the power balance can actually shift in favor of the wife. When a woman has a son who has been initiated, or a daughter who has married, she may talk back to, swear at, or even hit her husband (Hutchinson 1996: 183).

Ganwar and Nyapen were one of the few older Nuer couples in Minnesota—each being in their mid-thirties to early forties—and indeed the nature of their relationship was notably different from that of most husbands and wives. She openly laid down rules against his drinking, but also would relax these as a reward for good behavior. One day while interviewing Ganwar, I asked about Nuer husbands hitting their wives during quarrels. Nyapen, hearing this from across the room, shouted out, "Sometimes women hit their husbands," and everyone laughed. Her confidence, and the relative equality of their relationship, was striking. At the same time, this in no way diminished the status of

Ganwar. Quite the opposite, Ganwar was one of the most respected men in the community, known for his fairness and excellent manner in dealing with others.

CHANGING GENDER RELATIONS IN MINNESOTA

The ways that anthropologists understand gender relations has changed considerably in recent years. Until the past few decades, women's lives usually received little attention in anthropological accounts. The 1970s, however, saw a blossoming of an "anthropology of women" and a focus on the significance of women in a broad range of cultural contexts (Reiter 1975; Rosaldo and Lamphere 1974). These first waves of anthropological studies of women have been criticized by scholars for viewing women as a separate category for study, rather than an integral component of cultural groups (indeed, half or more of any population!). Increasingly, scholars seek to understand gender—including the full range of male and female identities and the relationships between men and women—as a pervasive part of all social and cultural activity (e.g., Collier 1988; Strathern 1988). Because of the significance of gender in defining social roles and relationships, any activity is necessarily closely intertwined with a culture's gender roles. Economic activities, for instance, cannot be fully understood without appreciating the sexual division of labor defined through the gender roles of men and women, or without taking into account household decision-making roles of husbands and wives.

Migration can be a particularly important context for redefining gender relations. Broad-ranging changes in daily life can bring major transformations not only in how men and women relate to each other, but also in how they see themselves. Among Korean immigrants for instance, economic life in the United States has drawn women into the outside labor force, in contrast to life in Korea where most stayed at home in a domestic role. As Korean women assume a more important economic role—and their husbands' economic status has frequently declined—significant marital tension and conflict often results (Min 1998). Similarly, Southeast

Asian women who have gone to work in meat packing plants in Kansas have found that access to an independent income can give them greater autonomy. This has resulted in women's greater assertiveness, but also higher rates of divorce, as well (Benson 1994).

How have Nuer gender roles and relationships been transformed in the United States? In Sudan, Nuer women and men have well-defined cultural roles that are integral to their daily life. The Nuer learn from childhood the particular tasks associated with their gender, as well as how men and women are expected to behave. Nuer children start to help around the home from an early age, and their work quickly becomes differentiated into male and female tasks. Boys learn that being a man means becoming responsible for herding cattle, and they gradually play a greater role in the care of livestock. Girls learn about cooking, milking, and taking care of the home, and see the importance of showing deference to men.

Male initiation is a key moment in instilling masculine ideals, as well as in emphasizing the culturally prescribed relationship between men and women. When a youth starts to show physical maturity and to leave childish behavior behind him, his parents will allow him to undergo initiation. Initiation usually takes place together with other boys, who as a group form an age set—*ric*—which will remain the most important peer group for their entire lives. Six incisions are made ear to ear across a boy's forehead, creating the scars of *gaar* which will mark his manhood.

Facing the knife without fear is considered by the Nuer to be their quintessential moment of self-mastery, which both defines their own manhood and differentiates them from Nuer women. This self-mastery comes to be expressed by many aspects of the behavior of a Nuer man—most importantly in regard to eating prohibitions. His relation to cattle should no longer be one in which he views livestock as a source of food, but rather one in which he has a paternalistic responsibility to oversee their well-being, to manage them for the good of the family, and to perform necessary cattle sacrifices. His relationship to cattle as food may only be mediated by the cooking of his food by a female relative. No matter how hungry, a man must not take food from an unrelated woman, nor prepare food for himself. He must not chew on both sides of his mouth, nor lick clean the sides of his bowl, lest he be subjected to public and private ridicule. To fail to adhere to these rules shows a lack of self-control, a lack of manliness (Hutchinson 1996).

With *gaar* a man gains the right to take part in cattle raids, but also the responsibility to protect the village from enemies and wild animals—responsibilities which he is expected to undertake without fear. Mastery over fear is seen as the key element which differentiates men from women in Nuer gender ideologies. Even Nuer men acknowledge that childbirth—the act which transforms a Nuer girl into a woman—is much more painful than their brief, if intense, encounter with the knife. Yet women cannot do so without fear—a point agreed upon by Nuer women, and not surprising given the high rates of maternal death. The perceived weakness of women associated with childbirth—along with the role of cattle sacrifice undertaken by men in protecting women and children—bolster male claims of physical and moral superiority over women (Hutchinson 1996).

There is significant separation of men and women, both in their daily activities and in the spaces they use. Men and women both take part in cultivation but have somewhat different roles. Women, for instance, may not use a digging stick for planting until they are past their childbearing years. Men are centrally concerned with the care of cattle, overseeing the herding operation, and doing some herding themselves. Women's work centers on the home and includes cooking, child care, and milking. Husbands do not spend a lot of time in the huts of their wives but rather prefer to be in the *luak*, with other men and with the cattle. The *luak* is the center of male collegiality, where men drink, smoke, talk, and often sleep. Huts (*dwil*), in contrast, are the center of female life.

These patterns do not necessarily translate well to life in the United States, where work is very different and where men and women need to cooperate in new ways. Power relations between men and women are also significantly altered in the United States. Ritual activities which justify male claims of superiority are absent, while Nuer women now encounter a social environment that promotes female independence rather than deference. Understandably, they may welcome this change, but it can cause significant stress within the marital relationship. Nuer men feel that women, who previously showed respect to men, no longer respect them.

Nuer couples are now forced closer together, both physically and in the organization of daily life. It is difficult to maintain distinct male and female spaces in Minnesota in the ways that the Nuer did in Sudan. Rather than living in spacious homesteads, spread out across the Sahelian landscape, with separate buildings for male and female activity, in Minnesota the Nuer live in small suburban apartments—usually with only one or two bedrooms for the entire family. Some men, at times, sleep separately from their wives, though this is difficult in such small apartments. When guests are present it is also common for women and men to go to separate parts of the home to socialize among themselves. For instance, men may go to a bedroom with their friends for drinking and conversation, while women and children remain in the living room. Alternatively, a woman might make herself scarce if her husband is socializing with his friends. Nevertheless, the kind of physical separation common in Sudan is simply not possible in Minnesota, and the Nuer frequently emphasize this change.

Differences in Nuer and American attitudes toward the closeness of the married couple are illustrated by an incident which occurred soon after the Nuer arrived in Minnesota. Several Nuer women became pregnant, and refugee agencies took steps to ensure that the Nuer—some of whom had given birth in Sudan, or in camps in Ethiopia or Kenya, using traditional Nuer midwifery—would make use of the medical facilities offered to them and give birth in the hospital rather than at home.

Most of the Nuer were ready, at least in principle, to accept this change. The public health nurses working with the Nuer women, however, felt that they needed some preparation for hospital birth so that they would be ready and know what to expect. This was particularly true for the first few Nuer women, since subsequent ones would be able to draw on their friends' experiences. The nurses who worked closely with the Nuer women decided to organize a field trip to the hospital, where the women could have a tour, see the facility, and learn about American birthing practices. Something always happened, though, and the field trip never took place—the van broke down, or the women couldn't go, or they were late to get ready.

As an alternative to the tour, the nurses decided that they would show the women an educational video which illustrated hospital birth. They gathered in the home of one of the Nuer women, and the two nurses and seven or eight Nuer women sat down to see the video which showed the hospital facilities, as well as an actual birth. Suddenly in the video a man appeared sitting on the bed of the woman in labor. "Who was this man?" they wondered, and when they realized that it was not a male doctor, but rather the woman's husband, the women exploded—some in uncontrollable laughter, others in terrified screams! Nuer men do not attend childbirth, and the very idea was alien and shocking to the women. The nurses tried to calm the women, explaining that their husbands did not have to be there, that many Americans believe that it is good for a husband to attend, but that it is a choice that they make themselves.

All was calm for some time, until the man appeared in the video again. This time, however, he did more than simply sit on the side of the bed. He leaned over his laboring wife, rubbed her head, and gave her a gentle kiss. With this, the women exploded even more uncontrollably than before, in laughter and in screams. One woman, eight months pregnant, leaped up, screaming; she ran out of the apartment, down two flights of stairs, out of the building and began running down the street! Fortunately one of the nurses retrieved the panicked mother-to-be. At this point the nurses sought out a Nuer man from the building who spoke English well enough to explain that their husbands need not be in the delivery room.

As one might imagine, Nuer women overwhelmingly have chosen not to have their husbands attend the birth, although one younger couple did eventually decide to have the husband there. This is an illustration—if an extreme one—of the rather different attitudes which Nuer and Americans have concerning male and female space and the relationship between men and women. If childbirth is increasingly seen in American culture as the ultimate moment of togetherness for a couple, to the Nuer it is the quintessential context for the separation of male and female spheres.

Although childbirth is an area where Nuer men and women are able to maintain the distinctness of male and female activities, the daily work of raising a family in Minnesota frequently requires couples to blur these boundaries and function as a single, cooperative unit. In Sudan, men and women had their own distinct tasks which they learned to master from the time they were children; in Minnesota there are many new tasks, with which neither men nor women are familiar, and performing old tasks in new contexts may force men and women to go outside of traditional gender roles. In Sudan, for instance, providing food is something which women do alone; in the United States men and women shop for food together. Nuer women are sometimes dependent on their husbands to perform tasks which would have been female work in Sudan, because they lack skills, such as competence in English or the ability to drive, necessary to perform these same tasks in the United States. If a woman needs to be at an appointment at a particular time, she might need to rely on her husband to drive her there, or else ensure that he will be home to watch the children while she is away. Where once men and women operated relatively independently of one another in organizing their daily lives, now they must cooperate in order to keep the family running smoothly.

The case of Kuany Thijok is a good example of the new standards of cooperation developing among the Nuer in this country. Not long after resettling in Minnesota, Kuany went to a friend's house for a weekend of drinking and visiting, leaving his wife alone at home with their daughter who was not feeling well. The child became seriously ill, and his wife—who was uncertain where Kuany was—had to deal with the situation herself. Lacking competence in English, she was unable to call the hospital herself, and the girl developed a dangerously high fever before a neighbor was finally able to help. When Kuany finally returned, he and his wife had a serious quarrel. Most of the Nuer in the community agreed that Kuany was wrong to act as he did, given the circumstances of life in the United States—a definite change from norms found in Sudan. There it would be common for men to go away visiting friends for periods of time. Women are able to handle most difficulties without assistance, and there are always neighbors, friends, and relatives nearby to help with any problems if need be. Here it is expected that men and women will act as a team, ready to provide help to one another in whatever ways are needed.

By and large, Nuer men have been placed in positions of far greater responsibility, both in terms of providing for the family and in terms of housework, than was the case in Sudan. In Sudan, both men and women do the work of cultivating the fields, while in the United States men are usually the ones expected to go out to find work in order to support their families. This is partly because men are more competent in English and because this is the model of work promulgated by American social service agencies. The Nuer also prefer that women care for infants and small children—a role which restricts them to the household in ways that it did not in Sudan, where women were able to combine child care with raising crops, collecting firewood, and performing other tasks.

When women in Minnesota do work, other kinds of stresses in gender roles can arise, as men are asked to perform home tasks that are outside the realm of normal gender expectations in Sudan. The most significant area in this regard is cooking. An important part of Nuer male initiation involves taking on strict rules concerning food and eating. Nuer men are expected to show no greediness in regard to food; they are not to milk cattle for themselves or to cook for their own consumption. The importance of these rules is so great that two of the scars of *gaar* on men's foreheads refer specifically to prohibitions against drinking milk oneself obtains from a cow—"Never again to suckle the udder" and "never again to lick milk froth from one's fingers" (Hutchinson 1996: p. 201). But if a woman works in Minnesota, she cannot also always be home to cook. Some Nuer men learned early in the resettlement process that the cooking prohibition could be quite difficult to adhere to in the United States, as they waited hungrily for their wives to return from working on the late shift. Many Nuer men have begun to cook in the United States, for themselves or their children, occasionally even with their wives present. Although this was initially a point of considerable tension, and still can be on some occasions, Nuer couples recognize that life in the United States sometimes requires a shift in gender responsibilities.

New and widely-accepted norms concerning the gender division of labor have not emerged among the Nuer in Minnesota. So far, it has mainly been a question of making adaptations as the need arises. In general, the Nuer have shown considerable flexibility. Working outside the home has predominantly been done by men, but neither men nor women express apprehension about women taking jobs. Women are sometimes employed—usually on a temporary basis in jobs like food processing—and their husbands may stay at home while they do. There is a preference for women looking after children, but men do so without complaint and without any sign that it diminishes their manhood. Tasks which require driving or greater English competence fall predominantly to men—but not, on the whole, because the Nuer feel that women should not do them, but because women have not yet acquired the necessary skills.

In some sense it is the lack of well-defined roles, as much as changes in roles, that causes tension within Nuer marriages in Minnesota. In Sudan there is no ambiguity about what is expected of a man and woman in marriage. This does not mean that conflict is absent, or that husbands and wives always fulfill their responsibilities. It does mean that there is common agreement about what constitutes a spouse's transgressions. Moreover, public opinion acts to bring the behavior of an erring husband or wife into accordance with Nuer norms and values. Men and women in Minnesota are consciously aware of their changing roles and understand the necessity of adjusting to new circumstances. If the positive side to this is flexibility, the negative side is that there may be little accord between husbands and wives about who *should* do what and about what each person's new responsibilities are.

Couples may draw on both Nuer and American discourses in arguing about male and female responsibilities in

Minnesota. One man commented on a problem his friend was experiencing:

> [My friend] is working and his wife is not working, and he [came home from work and] didn't get any food, and he tells his wife "Why you didn't cook and you are here and you are not working." And the wife say, "How can I cook and see my video? Can you comment on that? Leave your hunger in your car, yunno."

The wife's perceived transgression of not cooking is one in accordance with the traditional Nuer organization of domestic work. Yet the man's complaints were not framed in Nuer terms, but in accordance with new notions learned in the United States. He saw it as unfair that he should spend his days working, and then find that his wife had not taken responsibility for providing food. This position jibes with stereotypical images of the male American breadwinner expecting his dinner on the table after a hard day's work. The man did not raise an appeal to traditional Nuer explanations as to why her behavior would be wrong—that she should cook because it is a woman's job to cook.

Interestingly the man's response to this situation *did* draw on Nuer values. When he returned late from work and found that dinner had not been prepared for him, he decided simply to cook for himself. He did not do this because he felt that the responsibilities of men and women had changed in America—indeed, his reasons for cooking were quite the opposite. Cooking for himself under these circumstances— particularly because his wife was present—was wholly contrary to Nuer values and gender roles. By cooking he knew he would shame his wife and make her feel bad for what he saw as her laziness and inadequacy.

Men have more difficulty actually enforcing their desired pattern of household organization because their authority over their wives is greatly diminished in the United States. The idea that women in the United States are the equal of men was promoted even prior to resettlement, through cultural orientation programs held in Kenya to facilitate the adaptation of refugees. In the United States Nuer women have observed the freedom that American women enjoy and that a woman need not obey whatever a man says. They no longer see the need to follow their husband's orders—whether in the organization of work in the home or in making household expenditures—and can be quite assertive in expressing their views. Nuer men recognize that their own gender attitudes are out of step with American ideas. Indeed, they show no evidence of chauvinism towards American women. They do, however, have difficulty accepting that their own wives should be equal to them. In fact, some justify this double standard by saying that Nuer women are "too primitive" to handle freedom responsibly, having lived their whole lives in rural Africa and being monolingual in Nuer.

The most significant area of conflict within Nuer marriages is money. Coming from a background of subsistence agropastoralism—tilling the land and rearing livestock for the family's own consumption—the adjustment to the necessity of rent and the daily need for cash can be highly stressful. Although the Nuer often had access to money before leaving Sudan, or in Ethiopia, their basic needs were taken care of through farming, or pastoralism, or later through relief food supplied to them as refugees. Within this context, whatever money one had usually could simply be spent on nonessential items. The attitude that money is something to use on nonessential items was reinforced by expectations that coming to America meant wealth. Also, being in the United States and observing the consumer culture fuels desires for the things they see on television and in stores.

Despite these desires, Nuer incomes are quite low by American standards. When Nuer families have paid the rent and other bills, there is often little or nothing left. This lack of money can be a central focus for conflict. Men usually handle the money; women do not know exactly how much there is, or whether what their husbands say is true. If a husband claims that there is no money, women may question whether their husbands are hiding money for their own purposes. Conversely, men complain that women's material desires and expectations far outstrip their budgets and belie the inability of their (almost uniformly uneducated) wives to understand mathematical realities. One man complained of depression brought on by the constant demands of his wife to make various purchases, which were impossible because they were on welfare and had no money in the bank. More commonly, Nuer men express frustration that when women get money, they spend it on nonessential items before paying the bills.

The significance of money within gender conflict frequently goes beyond matters of household budgets. Arguments about money can, in fact, be deeply intertwined with the legitimacy of the marriage and the status and reputation of the woman, in particular. Because many relationships were formed in the context of displacement, traditional marriage—particularly full payment of bridewealth—has often not been completed. Even before the war, elopement had become increasingly common, although it was considered a shameful act, and was dealt with in government courts if the couple could be tracked down. If a couple in Minnesota does not send money to compensate for unpaid bridewealth, the wife risks being seen as little more than a wayward woman who has eloped and left her family without bridewealth, rather than a proper, married one.

In Minnesota, husbands and wives are both usually eager to remit money to kin remaining in Africa, but the recipients, amounts, and purposes of the remittances may be bitterly contested. Men wish to help their own families; women, for their part, not only want to assist those who stayed behind, but are also concerned that missing bridewealth is paid so that their status as married women is legitimized.

FROM DOMESTIC CONFLICT TO DOMESTIC VIOLENCE

The following folk tale, told to me—often quite spontaneously—by Nuer men, illustrates their views on domestic violence. Though there were some variations, the story goes roughly like this: A young wife went into the forest to collect firewood with the other village women. Chatting as they went, the conversation quickly turned to the beatings their husbands had given them, with each describing in turn the violent treatment they had received.

Everyone had a story to tell of this beating or that, or this fight or that, yet when it came to the young wife's turn all were aghast. Married for more than a year, she had never been beaten! The women wondered out loud what her life must be like, and what kind of man her husband must be, and the women quickly came together to remedy this situation. She must, they instructed, take her husband's ceremonial leopard skin and soil it. And when he knew it had been soiled she should throw it in the cooking fire. She went home and did this, and as the other village women had promised, her husband had no choice but to beat her.

Clearly, this story reflects a particularly male-centered point of view concerning domestic violence—that women have a need to be beaten. Nuer men say that women will not respect them if they go too long without being hit, that they will show improper behavior, and eventually will become unhappy in the company of such a weak man. Not surprisingly, Nuer women do not express the same sentiments. When I asked one Nuer woman about this tale, she laughed and responded simply "That is a man's history."

Nevertheless, it is clear that even in Sudan, Nuer marriages do not usually conform to American ideals of domestic bliss. While there may be considerable affection between husband and wife, conflict—not agreement—is considered the norm. In a quote now famous in anthropology, Evans-Pritchard discusses latent hostility between Nuer husbands and wives:

> Nuer have told me . . . that there is what we would call a latent antagonism between husband and wife and indeed between man and woman. They say that when a man has begotten several children by his wife he wants her to die, and may even pray for this to happen, for he does not want to die before her and another man to cohabit with her, rule in his home, use his cattle, and perhaps illtreat his children and rob them of their birthright. Men also say that in their hearts women wish for their husbands' deaths (1951: 133).

As I have shown, there are many new sources of stress—both individually and for couples—that the Nuer experience as refugees in Minnesota, and that may create even more conflict than would normally be found in Sudan. To make matters worse, the traditional context for conflict resolution—the broader kinship network—has diminished in significance. Other kin are frequently not present, and even when they are, their power to direct the couple is significantly less than in Sudan. They have generally not aided in the payment of bridewealth, and even if they had, this is meaningless within the American legal system. Within this context, domestic violence has emerged as a major problem.

Domestic violence is common even among the Nuer in Sudan. It is considered a man's right to hit his wife if he deems it necessary, and he may do so for a variety of reasons—for instance, failure to serve guests appropriately or to perform household tasks in a timely manner. While certainly one would not seek to justify the appropriateness of domestic violence in any context, its meaning is very different in traditional Nuer life than among Americans. Nuer men and women are both socialized in a cultural system in which violence is considered to be a normal part of marriage. Nuer women participate in the system by provoking and goading their husbands towards that outcome, questioning their strength and their manhood if they do not hit them, insulting them, and occasionally even becoming violent themselves [Hutchinson 1996; see also di Leonardo's (1979, 1991) discussion of evidence of female–male violence in Evans-Pritchard (1951: 103)]. Women do not, of course, wish to be beaten, but by verbally striking back at their husbands, they may assert their own power and demonstrate a lack of fear; if violence does result they can expect that others will intervene to resolve the underlying problems. Men and women are socialized to understand marriage as a context of conflict in which they exercise their differing opinions in a variety of ways, including domestic violence.

In the American context, domestic violence is simply illegal, and a spouse may be sent to jail for it. In cultural orientation programs and through social service agencies in the United States, Nuer women have been encouraged to "dial 911" if subjected to threats and/or domestic violence. Adapting to this new situation poses additional challenges to both Nuer men and women.

James Tap describes the experience of a friend who had quarrelled with his wife. Violence erupted, and the neighbors called the police. The friend was arrested. When asked about why he beat his wife, he explained that in Sudan a wife had to obey her husband; if she did not, it was his right to beat her. In response, the lawyer told him:

"This is America. The wife has freedom. If you have your own culture there, the wives are under control of you. But here it is different." And [the Nuer man] says "I pay a lot of cows there. She can follow my rules." And the lawyer told him "This is America. You are not still under Sudanese law. This is American law. Even if you pay a hundred cows there—you are in America. You can follow the American system that we do here."

"Dialing 911" has become a major issue between men and women in the Nuer community. Men realize that domestic violence is illegal in the United States and acknowledge that it is sometimes appropriate for women to seek police involvement in order to protect themselves from their husbands. What Nuer men complain about is that women use their ability to call the police as a weapon against their husbands in domestic disputes. One man in his thirties asserted, "If you just look at her [your wife] like you are serious, she dials 911." In general, Nuer men perceive that the political and legal context of American life has created a situation in serious contrast to Nuer values.

For one thing, Nuer men—and some women too—feel that the police, courts, and other government agents are biased in favor of women, for whom they become advocates in the context of domestic conflict. As one Nuer man complained, "The police only care if you hit your wife, but they don't care about all the things she might have done." In saying this he is not arguing that she *deserves* to be hit, but rather that wives may do things to cause the conflict, or do things in the course of conflict, which both Nuer men and women consider far worse than hitting—for example, insulting her husband, demeaning his manhood, being intentionally neglectful of the home, or repeatedly committing adultery. The police, they say, are interested only if the conflict results in violence. This does not mean that women's actions are believed to *justify* violence—not necessarily even to Nuer men. Rather, Nuer men and women perceive violence as arising out of patterns of mutual contestation and conflict within the home; violence is sometimes a natural outgrowth of these circumstances, not the only bad thing, or even the worst thing, that men and women can do to one another. By privileging violence over other negative behavior, the Nuer see the government as providing advocacy for women, rather than seeking a fair resolution of disputes.

An important difference in Nuer and American attitudes towards domestic violence is the emphases on how it should be dealt with. American social workers and police place the safety of the woman above all, and they seek to remove a woman from a violent situation and prevent violence from reoccurring. The Nuer, in contrast, are most concerned with preserving the marriage and family. One Nuer man said that in America, as in Sudan, "When a man and woman argue, the first thing she says is that she is going," and yet the implications of this are very different. In Sudan, she will go to stay with her parents or other members of her natal family. In doing so, her husband or his brothers will be forced to go after her and convince her kin that whatever problems existed between them will be addressed and that any mistreatment will stop. The husband may also seek guarantees that misbehavior on her part will stop. Her kin will generally wish to successfully negotiate her return, both in the interests of the couple and because they will need to return 25 cattle if the separation turns into divorce. In contrast, when a Nuer woman leaves her husband in the United States, she frequently ends up in a woman's shelter. Her husband may not even be welcome there, and institutional factors may work against her return. In most cases in Minnesota, Nuer women who have gone to shelters have decided to return to their husbands—often after having many Nuer men and women visit to encourage them to preserve their families. The whole process, however, can itself be quite damaging to Nuer marriages, with Nuer men being apprehensive about the return of their wives after the course of negative events. A man may feel that the situation started with mistreatment at the hands of his wife, only to lead to being sent to jail when he responded to her behavior by hitting her.

The Nuer practice of bridewealth payments complicates matters. One reason for men's resentment when police and social workers encourage their wives to leave them is that many have paid substantial amounts of bridewealth to their wife's family, even if they have not completed the full payment. For some, this has meant great expense and hardship, yet in the United States, they find, it means nothing. In Sudan, if there was a conflict and a wife left, a man could go to her family and have the bridewealth returned. Yet as one man pointed out angrily at a meeting to discuss these issues, if the police or women's shelter takes away his wife, they will not give him back his cows in return.

Problems with domestic violence have abated somewhat since the main fieldwork period in the late 1990s. This seems to be due less to a substantive reworking of gender relationships and forms of interaction between husbands and wives than to a realization on the part of men that the consequences of hitting their wives can be severe. As one man put it in noting that domestic violence had abated "Men have learned." Interestingly, the Nuer's own reactions to the problem of domestic violence owe little to cultural relativism, and the subtle attention to cultural dynamics, which anthropologists typically apply to culture change. Although anthropologists would not defend a practice such as violence against women, they would generally prescribe understanding the social dynamics that produce it, and seek a remedy which works within those dynamics. The Nuer community's own responses have been exactly the opposite—heavy-handed messages that this cultural practice must stop. Thus, for instance, in 2001, the Nuer produced an educational video concerning domestic violence. The video featured a Nuer man and Nuer woman, explaining that domestic violence is against the law in the United States, while seated on either side of a uniformed police officer. The height and position of the chairs completely distorted the relative size of the policeman and the Nuer, so that the considerably shorter officer appeared massive, dwarfing the Nuer man, who was well over six feet tall. The subtext to the video was none too subtle: Hit your wife and this mountain of a man will come to get you. When I met the officer, he was very much aware that this was the point the Nuer wanted to convey, and mentioned that there had even been a slight disagreement with the Nuer producing the video. They had strongly wanted him to wear his gun for added effect, but this was against police department policy.

Violent disputes at times have resulted in divorce among Nuer couples in Minnesota, which is another arena where Nuer practices and the American legal system are at odds. In Nuer culture, any children resulting from a marriage belong to a man, and stay with him in the event of divorce. Infants who are still nursing and other very small children will generally stay with their mother until they are older and less dependent on her. Transferring rights in children from the wife's family to the husband's family is, indeed, one of the most important functions of the payment of bridewealth. In Sudan, a Nuer divorce generally results in the return of bridewealth cattle; the number of cows which need to be returned is dependent on the number of children the wife has bore for her husband. If the number of children is already substantial—perhaps three or four—no cattle may need to be returned, since the husband and his kin are thought to have received the children for which bridewealth was paid (Hutchinson 1996). Thus, children will stay with the husband and his kin, rather than go with the wife if she leaves.

The fact of children remaining with the husband is a major factor in contributing to the stability of Nuer marriages in Sudan. Knowing that they will need to abandon their children to abandon their husband—and fearing mistreatment of their children at the hands of a stepmother—dissuades Nuer women from leaving their marriage. When Hutchinson mentioned that in America children often remain with their mothers after divorce, one Nuer woman responded:

> Oh, we Nuer thought of that [possibility] long ago but rejected the idea because, if the children were to remain with the mother, all wives would leave their husbands—and so, with us, its always the father who keeps them (1996: 183–184).

The American legal system, in contrast, tends to favor women when awarding custody of children in divorce hearings. While joint custody, as well as custody for the father, is becoming more common in American courts, the traditional model of having children live with the mother still predominates. The fact that Nuer divorce in Minnesota is often preceded by domestic violence clearly works against awarding custody to the father. When this occurs, Nuer men are very bitter, arguing that they have paid a substantial number of cattle (or its cash equivalent) for rights to their children, only to have them capriciously taken away from them without compensation.

The economic value of children within the American welfare system sometimes renders them pawns in their parents' divorce proceedings. Most Nuer families remain highly dependent on welfare, and children are the key to access to most programs. Without children it is difficult to qualify, and each additional child increases one's entitlement. If a woman successfully leaves with her children, she takes with her the family's principal source of income. Simon Luoth and his wife Nyakat Dung illustrate this process. They had been married in Ethiopia in the early 1990s and had three children. They came to Minnesota in 1994, and lived in the northern suburbs. After a time, they began to quarrel frequently, particularly concerning money. These quarrels led to physical violence and police intervention, with Simon spending the night in jail and Nyakat going to a women's shelter. Because neither one of them worked regularly (though both sometimes did temporary work), their main income was from welfare. When Nyakat left with the children, Simon was no longer able to pay rent, and was forced to live with friends. Because money had been the principal source of quarrels, Nyakat was happy to have complete control of the family's income. Simon was not happy about this turn of events and sought return of the children, both because of his need for income and as a way to gain leverage over his estranged wife. He was, however, unsuccessful.

DISCUSSION

The discussion in this chapter provides a rather bleak picture of Nuer marriage and gender relations in Minnesota. Conflict is common, frequently resulting in domestic violence and sometimes divorce. Yet while there are many problems, there are also many successes. There are many instances in which flexibility and the readiness to adapt to changed circumstances have enabled the Nuer to successfully reforge their families. If the problems between Simon and Nyakat led to violence and separation, other couples such as Buol and Nyabuom have faced the same problems and managed to maintain the peace and unity of their families. Even serious conflicts do not necessarily spell the end of a marriage, but may—as is often the case in Sudan—lead to changes in the behavior of one or both parties. Even Simon and Nyakat continued to meet—secretly because of a restraining order imposed against Simon—to find a way to preserve their family. There is, perhaps, cause for optimism in the fact that the Nuer have recognized the problems that domestic violence poses in the United States and that they have taken up active discussion among themselves of ways that they might mediate domestic problems in the absence of a well-defined kinship network.

Children's Issues

At about 3 P.M. Nyalan arrives home from the middle school in a neighboring suburb, where she is bused because English as a Second Language classes are not offered in her home district. Dressed in baggy jeans, platform shoes, and a short tee shirt which exposes her midriff, there is little visually to distinguish her from an African-American girl her age—of whom there are few at her school, but many more to emulate on the TV which is nearly always on in her home. Nylan's father died while she was still in Africa. When her brother, Kuach, got permission to come to the United States, she and her younger brother came along to live with him, his wife Nyapak, and their children.

Like Nyalan, Nuer children and youth face a considerable challenge in successfully negotiating an unfamiliar social and academic environment in school while at the same time maintaining a positive family life at home—often in the absence of the birth parents. More than their parents, school-age children and youth are constantly engaged with American culture.

Nuer teenagers often have a lot of responsibility around the home, cleaning, running errands, or taking care of younger siblings, as pictured here.

Every day they enter an educational system based on American culture and the English language, only to return at the end of the day to a Nuer home life in which Nuer is spoken exclusively and which is organized around cultural values and practices very different from American ones.

PARENTAL GUIDANCE

Nuer and American parenting styles differ significantly, fostering different types of skills in children. While American parenting tends to emphasize high levels of parent–child interaction, with close attention to a child's every need, Nuer parents tend to promote independence and self-sufficiency in children from a very young age. Both men and women are quite loving and affectionate towards their children. At the same time, their parenting style is looser than that of most Americans in many ways. Typically they let children do things for themselves and find out for themselves how things work. Rather than showing or explaining skills to children directly, they expect children will learn on their own or by observing other children.

The results of these differing styles were evident in comparing the development of my own daughter, Clare, with that of several Nuer children of about the same age. Clare was only four months old when I began working with the Nuer, and she frequently accompanied me to Nuer homes. In many ways the development of Nuer children left Clare far behind; they could sit and play independently months ahead of her, run when she was just starting to walk, and successfully complete toilet training before their second birthday. At the same time, the Nuer were frequently surprised at Clare's ability to express herself verbally in much more complex sentences than Nuer toddlers her age. This led to a rather telling interaction with Buol, whose daughter Nyanuar was just a week older than Clare. Inquiring with curiosity about how she had developed her verbal skills Buol asked, "Is it because you talk to her every day?" I was surprised at his question: Of course I spoke to her every day. Didn't Buol speak to Nyanuar every day? Buol was more attuned to differences in our parenting styles than I was, noting that when he spoke to his daughter, it was to tell her to do something, or to direct her on how to behave, rather than to speak just for the sake of speaking. While I spent a great deal of time trying to encourage and teach Clare to speak and understand, Buol focused more on directing his daughter in ways which would help her deal with her physical and social world herself.

In Nuer homes, children and adults tend to operate in very different spheres. Frequently, adults eat at different times than the children, though small children may join their parents in search of tidbits from their bowls. While adults cook, eat, or talk, children will play or watch television around them, playing with relatively more freedom than American children typically do. In general, Nuer children come and go between apartments, and sometimes go outside on their own without a great deal of supervision. In Sudan, the Nuer note, even quite small children wander about very freely in the proximity of the village—with parents principally concerned only that they stay away from nearby rivers. In the United States, however, the Nuer have learned that cars and other hazards make it necessary to keep children inside, at least until they are old enough to play safely. Consequently, the Nuer perceive the level of interaction between parents and children—even if minimal by American standards—is comparatively intense to what they are accustomed to in Sudan. Disciplining children has changed significantly in the United States. In Sudan, corporal punishment is frequently used to control children's behavior, yet in the United States social workers have emphasized that the Nuer should not beat their children. The Nuer also express fear that a child might dial 911 if he or she were hit. Certainly, corporal punishment has not entirely ceased, but many have sought to severely curtail it.

The Nuer feel that in following these prescriptions, children lose respect for their parents, are rude, and do not listen and obey. As I talked to Buol and his wife about disciplining children, Nyanuar went to the refrigerator and opened it, despite being admonished not to. Buol laughed at the example which suddenly presented itself and noted:

> If she was beaten, tomorrow she would not repeat it again. But because she is not beaten, she does it always. Just by talking, she couldn't understand.

OLDER CHILDREN AND YOUTH

Relatively few teenagers arrived in Minnesota compared to the overall Nuer population. Because the majority of Nuer arrivals in Minnesota were young adults, most were not old enough to have teenage children. Some teenage boys did flee Sudan without their parents or went to Kenya alone in order to apply for resettlement, but these teenagers, by now, have matured into young men. However, a small number of teenagers who traveled to Minnesota, either as unaccompanied minors, accompanied by older siblings, or in a few instances with one or both parents. By and large, these (mostly male) teenagers came without guardians.

Teenage boys without parents generally live together in groups of three to five, both to split living expenses and for the sake of companionship. While they are eligible for some cash assistance—particularly before they are eighteen or finish high school—this is generally not enough to meet their needs for living expenses and a little spending money. Most work part-time to make extra money at the same time as they are going to school.

Since the initial years after resettlement, youth issues have become a growing source of tension in Nuer communities in Minnesota and elsewhere, as the many Nuer children who came with their parents in the 1990s are now in full-blown adolescence. These earlier refugees have been joined, as well, by a large contingent of mostly male youths and young men, as the remaining 3,000 "Lost Boys" were resettled in the United States in 2001–2002. Compared to refugees who came as adults, this younger generation is typically less oriented towards memories of life in Africa, and places relatively less importance on Nuer culture than the American lifestyle that has dominated their growing up. As Koth, a Nuer man now in his 40s, described the attitudes of most teenagers: "They think 'I'll just do it the American way,'" without heed to their cultural background, or the views and values of their parents. Becoming "more American," as many sociologists have noted, is not necessarily positive. Increasingly, Nuer youth have become involved in negative aspects of American youth culture, such as drugs, gangs, and teen pregnancy, at the expense both of educational success and Nuer values.

The lack of parental supervision sometimes results in various behavioral problems. In urban Nuer communities, such as Omaha, problems such as gang activity, drugs, shoplifting, and other forms of theft have become a growing problem for Nuer youth, while in Minnesota drinking has been a major issue. Nuer youth are traditionally not allowed to drink, but in the absence of adults to control this behavior, it is not uncommon for drinking problems to develop. At times, cousins or uncles may step in to try to mitigate behavioral problems, though their authority is more limited than that of a parent.

Seventeen-year-old Kayier is a Nuer youth who lived with seven friends and cousins in two apartments in a suburban complex. After a time, Kayier started to associate with a group of Nuer teenagers who were involved in theft and substance abuse, and he began to take part in these activities. He also got into a fight at school, and was suspended for several days. When the group of youth with whom he had been getting into trouble decided to move to another state, his roommates were concerned when they learned that Kayier planned to go with them. On the night that Kayier intended to leave, his roommates, along with two older cousins, forbade him to go and physically prevented him from joining his troublesome friends. Kayier was, needless to say, very upset and threatened to call the police if his roommates wouldn't release him. He finally demurred when they agreed that he could move to the other state when some other relatives moved there in a few weeks' time.

Kayier was lucky, to the extent that he had other Nuer looking out for him who sought—if not always with complete success—to keep him on a straight path. Other Nuer youth have been less fortunate. Several have spent some time in local jails for a variety of offenses, such as theft and underage drinking.

School

Nuer children and youth have varying experiences in American schools. School is an environment alien to anything young Nuer have ever experienced, who either had no formal education at all, or a very different kind of formal education in refugee camps in Ethiopia or Kenya. Even so, educators and social workers have been amazed that most of the Nuer children and youth have not had major problems adjusting to a suburban school environment. While two months before they may have been living in the refugee camps, they quickly became, for the most part, comfortable and effective students in the United States.

Problems can arise for a number of reasons. English is an issue for all of them. Moreover, many children and youth had little or no formal schooling before arriving in Minnesota. While schools find it necessary to place Nuer students in classes appropriate to their age and social and physical development, this may be out of step with their academic readiness. This can cause difficulties for students and schools alike. Nyakan, for instance, is about twelve years old, but quite tall and physically mature for her age. She was doing well academically in an elementary school as a fifth grader, but the school felt that there were social problems associated with her being somewhat older and much larger than the other fifth graders. Nyakan was transferred to a middle school, but she had trouble adjusting academically, and this resulted in behavioral problems as well.

The high mobility of Nuer refugees can also pose problems for Nuer students. Families and individuals move often, either to other states or to alternate housing within the metropolitan area. As a consequence, Nuer students frequently do not stay in the same school for prolonged periods of time, making it difficult for them to adjust to that particular school environment and for schools to understand their particular needs. When moves occur during the school year—as they frequently do—the disruption to learning can be all the more significant.

Nuer children and youth intermingle with American students to varying degrees. At the lower grade levels, intercultural friendships are fairly common, and younger Nuer children may spend time with American friends in school and after school. Relationships with Americans are usually less significant in the higher grades. Many older students are busy because they work as well as go to school. They may legally be as old as 21, and (because of inaccuracies in their travel documents) some may be even older, so that they have little in common with high school students. Generally they interact with the handful of other Nuer students within the school—in classes, at lunch, in the halls, and the like—and have little contact with American students after the school day is over. Scarification is found on many older male students—both the *gaar* of initiation on the forehead, and the decorative *bir* in geometric patterns on the face—which makes them stand out and undoubtedly adds to the difficulties in being fully accepted by Americans in a high school environment. Nuer youth are generally highly motivated to do well, however, and tend to get decent grades, although classes which require high English proficiency can be problematic. As they struggle to succeed in school, Nuer youth have several goals. They know that education is a key to getting a good job and to success in the United States. They also are aware of the prestige that an American diploma would bring them if peace should come to Sudan, and they have the opportunity to return there. I worked with a group of American teens in developing a friendship/mentoring program with Nuer children and youth. The program aimed to promote interaction between the Nuer and Americans and to aid the adjustment of Nuer youth to American life and American schools. While no long-lasting friendships emerged—and the logistics of providing transportation for 20 or more Nuer youth could be vexing to say the least—when things went well, there were beautiful moments of intercultural understanding. Among the most memorable was a sledding party which my wife and I held at our house, attended by about 20 American teenagers and about the same number of Nuer children and youth. From the standpoint of an anthropologist steeped in the romantic mystique of the Nuer, cultivated in a half century of academic tradition, it was an occasion for profound irony. The group of Nuer varied widely in age, from perhaps ten years old to young men who, though still in high school, were as old as their early twenties. Standing on the hill overlooking Minnehaha Creek, I could not quite decide what to make of the image of these young Nuer men—who in the anthropological imagination should be taking up spears to raid cattle from their Dinka neighbors—skittering joyously on toboggans down the wintry slope.

The real interaction, though, occurred inside. Amidst the fruit, the junk food, and the massive pots of gallons of hot cocoa needed to restore life to frozen extremities, spontaneous moments of intercultural friendship quickly took shape. The stereo played and Americans, and then Nuer, took to the dance floor, joined shortly by my daughter Clare's very large stuffed monkey, which they spun and tossed between one another. In these moments I was moved to see Nuer and American youth interacting with each other not as "Nuer and Americans" or "refugees and native borns" or "those-in-need and those-providing-help," but simply as a group of young people coming together to have a good time.

Starting Families in the United States

What about those who are at a different life stage and who are starting families of their own? Due to the unbalanced gender ratio among the Nuer in the Twin Cities, starting a family is a problem for many young men. If a young man was unmarried when he came to the United States, it may be difficult to get married once here. There are few unmarried Nuer women in the United States and only a handful of older teenage girls. While young Nuer men are content to date American women, in most cases they hope to marry another Nuer.

One solution is to marry a girl who is still in Africa (usually in Ethiopia) and then to get permission to bring her to the United States. This can be extremely difficult. Usually, the Immigration and Naturalization Service (INS) only allows wives to join husbands if they were listed as family members on their husband's original application for resettlement. Thus, even if a man marries a woman in Africa, it may be difficult for her to rejoin him in the United States. Because there are few other alternatives, however, young men continue to attempt this route.

In early 1997, James Tap traveled to Ethiopia in order to get married. He was making a relatively high wage working at a hotel in Minneapolis, and by saving scrupulously was able to raise the $6,000 required to pay for his travel, to buy presents for family members, and to cover the expenses of the marriage ceremony. His family had already selected a bride for him and made all the arrangements with her family. Indeed when he arrived in Addis Ababa, he was so busy meeting friends and relatives and making travel and visa arrangements that the marriage ceremony was held back at the village without him! While this may seem strange from an American point of view, it is less so to a Nuer. Because a marriage is between families, the presence of the man himself, while desirable, is not essential. This is illustrated by the traditional Nuer practice of "ghost marriage" in which a bride is married to a dead son so that she might bear children in his name. It was almost a year before James and his wife were actually together. He was not immediately able to get permission for her to come to the United States and was forced to return alone. It was not until early 1998 that she made it to Minnesota.

Increasingly marriage, sexuality, and starting families have also come to be issues among Nuer girls in the United States, who arrived as children and have moved into their teenage years or beyond. But in the initial years following resettlement there were very few teenage girls, and these few were still highly enculturated in Nuer life, and seemingly quite comfortable with marrying according to Nuer customs. Thus, for instance, in 1998, two Nuer teenage girls in Minnesota moved to other states where they married young Nuer men. In both cases the girls were young by American standards. One girl was only 14 or 15, the other only slightly older. These ages are, however, normal by Nuer standards; a girl is considered marriageable by the time she reaches sexual maturity. It should be noted that in these two cases what occurred was more akin to betrothal than actual marriage because the girls have continued to live with their parents.

The marriages of these two girls involved only one of the three distinct ceremonies in Nuer marriage. The three ceremonies are termed *larcieng* (betrothal), *ngut* (marriage), and *mut* (consummation). The larcieng betrothal ceremony is considered optional and was not performed for the girls married from Minnesota. The mut consummation ceremony also may not take place for some time because the girls are still young. The ngut marriage ceremony was performed although not in a fully traditional way because slaughtering an ox is the key act in the marriage, and live oxen are not available to urban Nuer. Normally the blood of the slaughtered ox forms the covenant between husband and wife.

It is not possible to pay bridewealth cattle in the United States, where cash is paid instead. Cash bridewealth payments are substantial; in one instance it was $10,000 with $6,000 paid immediately and another $4,000 to be paid later. This is more than couples, who had not fully married before coming to the United States sent to families in Africa to buy bridewealth cattle. In these cases, $100 to $200 per cow was adequate, so that total payment was between $2,500 and $5,000. The fact that there were so few marriageable Nuer girls in the United States undoubtedly contributed to bridewealth inflation here. The Minnesota families that received bridewealth for their teenage girls used the money to purchase a car and other items; some was sent to relatives in Africa who needed assistance and who were entitled to a share of bridewealth.

In these early marriages the girls were apparently comfortable with the marriages. Moreover, they were happy about being able to help their families in such a major way and, as for their families, the receipt of such substantial bridewealth was a source of considerable pride. Their worth could be quantified, and it was two to four times that of most Nuer girls in Sudan! More recently, however, Nuer girls have increasingly decided that they will "Just do it the American way." This has led to tensions between parents and daughters, who often do not wish to be married off by their parents, and have their own—new—ideas about dating and teen pregnancy.

In traditional Nuer culture premarital sex is not uncommon, but within a somewhat regulated framework, particularly in regard to girls. In Sudan, brothers and parents commonly monitor the activities of girls, and seek to avoid an appearance of promiscuity that would damage the reputations of both the girl and her family. In addition to seeking to regulate the activities of girls within their families, fathers and brothers can confront boyfriends or the boys' families to protect a girl's and her family's reputation. Moreover, should a pregnancy result, the boyfriend is expected to pay a fine and/or marry the girl.

The dynamics of the American context are, however, considerably different. Many parents are loath to allow their teenagers—particularly teenage daughters—to date, but may have little power to prevent it. Parents are unable to monitor their teenagers constantly, and there are many contexts that allow teenagers to escape supervision entirely. Because of their busy schedules many Nuer parents are often not at home. Also, many young men and male teenagers do not have parents in the United States, and share apartments with other young men without parental supervision. Parents, moreover, may have very limited ability to exercise control of their children of either gender, particularly in comparison with how things are in Sudan. This can lead to a variety of problems, including increasing incidents of teen pregnancy. Consider, the case of Nyabuol, a girl in her mid-teens. She began to skip school, frequently spending her days at her boyfriend's apartment. Although he was living with his parents, they were frequently not at home, and the apartment was a meeting point for many teenagers. When Nyabuol's father found out what was going on, he complained to the young man's father that he needed to control his son, as he might have in the Sudanese context. In the United States, however, it was to little effect, except to lead to considerable tension between the two men, as the boy's father asserted that he had little power over his son. Nyabuol's father also tried to curtail Nyabuol's activities directly, but if anything, these efforts backfired. She ended up running away with a different young man to another state, where she became pregnant and had a child.

Dating and adolescent sexuality thus can be a major source of tension between parents and children. The tensions are exacerbated by cultural barriers which make it difficult for parents to talk to their children about birth control if they are going to be sexually active. On occasion, conflicts over dating have become violent, leading to charges of child abuse against some Nuer parents. In the years since resettlement began, Nuer men have increasingly learned that domestic violence against their wives can result in severe legal consequences, but Nuer parenting styles that have long relied on corporal punishment have been more durable. Several cases of alleged abuse have involved the efforts of Nuer parents to forcibly marry their teenage daughters who have become pregnant. If a girl becomes pregnant, marriage is the natural outcome from a Nuer perspective, and the fact that forced marriage is unacceptable in the American context—and can even lead to criminal charges against the parents—is frustrating and paradoxical to many Nuer parents. As one Nuer father said in exasperation at a community meeting on family issues: "You let your daughter date. You let your daughter have sex and get pregnant. But if you want her to get married this is abuse." Thus, on the one hand, he is struck by what he sees as neglect and laxity in parental responsibility in the United States, where it is acceptable for parents to allow children to do as they please. Yet when parents act in what he sees as a responsible manner—for instance, by insisting that their pregnant daughters get married—they are stigmatized, or even criminalized.

CONCLUSION

In some senses, family issues have become even more important to the Nuer in Minnesota than they were in Sudan. While the family has always been a crucial unit for the Nuer, around which social and economic aspects of their daily life revolved, in Sudan any family was but one hub in an intricate web of social relations defined by village and kinship. Even if the family was the most immediate point of that web for any individual, it was only one point, and it was defined by its connections to a broader network. That the Nuer now live apart from this kinship network, in largely self-sufficient nuclear families, changes the significance of family relationships in a host of ways.

On one hand, the nuclear family is now paramount. Ties between husbands and wives, and parents and children, are by far the most crucial ones in the Minnesota Nuer community, as broader kin ties are largely absent. In Minnesota, a couple may be left alone to resolve their issues without the aid of concerned relatives who have a tangible stake in their continued well-being. There is much comfort which the Nuer in Minnesota may take from their family, as a point of continuity and support in a radically different world, but at the same time they must rework the forms and the meanings of family relationships in the United States.

6

Nuer Refugees in the American Community

"They are the most genuine people I have ever met," says Linnea, a woman who worked closely with the Nuer for over two years and spoke of the way they provided her with the purest "unconditional friendship." In almost direct contrast, another American, Earl, left his volunteer work disappointed and disillusioned with the Nuer who he felt were simply trying to take advantage of him for material gain. As Linnea and Earl illustrate, the relationship between the Nuer and Americans is complex, and in many ways a study in contradictions. Where one person perceives total openness, another perceives deceit.

To a great extent, the nature of interactions between the Nuer and Americans are context dependent, varying widely according to the type of "mediating institutions" (Lamphere 1992), which bring the Nuer and Americans together—social service agencies, hospitals, churches, and the like. Each situation brings with it a very different underlying material and social context which shapes the goals and perceptions of both the Nuer and Americans involved in the interaction. At the same time, understandings of one another affect the nature of relations between Americans and the Nuer, while the outcomes of their interactions sometimes reinforce—but also sometimes begin to change—these understandings.

Nuer ties to the American community are not, in fact, very intense. The social ties of Nuer refugees to one another are much more important. Fellow Nuer share a common background and common experiences of life in rural Africa, values derived from Nuer culture, and most importantly, the Nuer language which remains the primary, and most comfortable, mode of communication for most of the Nuer in Minnesota. While Nuer language, values, and culture are a source of comfort and security, they do not provide common ground with the Americans they encounter. Nuer friendships, therefore, tend to center on a network of other Nuer.

Needless to say, however, the Nuer cannot live in America and be part of an American community while avoiding those who make up the bulk of its members. Even if some Nuer are not interested in forging friendships or other ties with Americans, they inevitably have dealings with Americans in a variety of contexts—in schools, health care, rental housing, and employment, to name a few. In addition, many Nuer have become involved in Twin Cities churches, which are a critical setting for interactions with Americans.

THE AMERICAN COMMUNITY AND ITS RESPONSE

November 1994 saw a sudden, unexpected influx of Nuer refugees into the northern suburbs of the Twin Cities. The few Nuer who had already arrived in Minnesota had gone largely unnoticed, but this new wave was rather dramatic. The Nuer—drawn to Minnesota by reports from their friends, but not necessarily with any definite plans—were showing up at the bus station, without any place to live. The county was suddenly faced with a burgeoning population with potentially serious homelessness and health problems, but little or no competence in English.

The possible impact of these new, African refugees on the host community was uppermost in the minds of many local residents and government officials. The communities in which they were resettled were predominantly white—mainly whites of Scandinavian or German descent, who were the predominant ethnic group in Minnesota. The suburban fringe communities of the Twin Cities metropolitan area are largely urban, but they have a homogenous, white, Nordic feel, not unlike the rural Minnesota familiar to many Americans through Garrison Keilor's parodies of the mythical town of Lake Wobegone. Frequently, sites such as these have been favored by resettlement agencies for refugee placement. It is assumed that in relatively homogeneous communities new arrivals will not immediately be stereotyped with local minority populations and become victims of pre-existing prejudices. While refugees may be able to start with a "clean slate," the problem with homogeneous communities is that they are often more uncomfortable with diversity, and less prepared to deal with it effectively, than places that are already diverse.

Aware of these potential difficulties, Anoka County took a number of steps. A particular concern was how social services would deal with the burden of the sudden and unexpected arrival of the Nuer. Two staff members were hired to specifically work with the Nuer—not just to help the Nuer with their special problems, but also to mitigate potential disruption to the community and, in particular, social service agencies. English as a Second Language classes were quickly expanded for the Nuer, and Public Health Nurses were assigned to focus on work with the Nuer. While none of these people knew much about Nuer culture, they had some experience with other international populations, including Africans; most chose to work with the Nuer (rather than being assigned that work) because of an interest in other cultures and a desire to help people they saw as being particularly disadvantaged. They brought an openness and enthusiasm for other cultures to the job that allowed them to establish good relationships with the Nuer and became well integrated into the Nuer community as reliable sources of assistance, often going beyond their job requirements to help.

It is striking that local residents and government agencies mobilized so quickly—and hired two full-time workers—to deal with only a few hundred Nuer. Perhaps this was due in part to the shock of the sudden influx of Nuer, and the uncertainty of how large the Nuer migration would become. With a few hundred Nuer arriving in a few months, Americans foresaw the possibility that there might soon be thousands. The Nuer also stood out in the Twin Cities and, by all measures, were particularly in need of assistance. They were rural Africans in a frigid, urban environment; they were refugees from a brutal civil war; and they were Christians fleeing the oppression of Muslim rulers.

It was not only the county government which mobilized to help the Nuer; voluntary organizations also stepped in to help. One church became a repository for clothing and other items donated to aid the Nuer. So many donations were given that the church soon ran out of room to store them—there were simply more people giving than there were Nuer to receive. Monthly meetings were also held at the church to coordinate efforts among the many government and voluntary agencies assisting the Nuer. Particularly in the early stages of resettlement, it was common to find 30 to 40 or more Americans in attending these meetings, along with a handful of Nuer. Some Americans who attended the meetings were simply interested individuals, but more often they were representatives of larger organizations or churches which were in some way engaged in work with the Nuer.

UNDERSTANDING THE NUER

Coming to an understanding of who the Nuer are can be difficult for Minnesotans who have little experience with African populations. Minnesotans generally refer to the Nuer as "Sudanese," emphasizing national identity rather than the ethnic category, which is most meaningful to the Nuer themselves. Particularly in the early days of the resettlement process, Americans had difficulty understanding why being Nuer was much more important than being Sudanese—national identity, however, was largely a creation of borders drawn by European colonial powers. Americans were disappointed by the lack of solidarity and cooperation between all southern Sudanese. One ESL teacher tried to foster a friendship between a Nuer child and another Sudanese child and found that they not only couldn't understand each other, but they seemed to have an instant dislike for each other.

Americans often have a great deal of interest in Nuer culture and want to know what life was like in Sudan. The Nuer who are in close contact with Americans are frequently called on to give presentations at schools, churches, men's clubs, and other kinds of meetings, focusing both on traditional Nuer life and their experiences as refugees. On occasion, this has included a presentation of Nuer singing and dancing, as well. One Sunday morning a group of about a dozen Nuer men and women was asked to provide entertainment for the International Day brunch of an upscale, all white, suburban church. The Nuer had not brought their traditional dance regalia from Sudan, but they were able to put together some beads and other decorations. The Nuer, who have few opportunities for these kinds of cultural expressions, enjoyed themselves immensely, whooping, dancing, and singing energetically as their dance lines circulated among the American families who were sitting down to pancakes and sausages in their Sunday best.

Although Americans express an interest in Nuer culture, what concerns them most is the Nuer's need to assimilate to American life, especially in the area of language. Many Americans see the Nuer's continued emphasis on speaking their own language as detrimental. While most Nuer are studying English, either in special ESL classes or in formal school, they do not use English when speaking with other Nuer. "Don't you think they need to speak English at home?" asked Vera, a woman who did volunteer work in Nuer ESL classes at a local church. In her opinion, the classes alone were not sufficient to provide the kind of English competence necessary for the Nuer to thrive in their new lives as Americans. Thus, while Vera, like many Americans working with the Nuer, had a respect for and interest in Nuer culture, she also felt that the Nuer's desire to associate mainly with one another and converse in their own language was harmful to successful assimilation into American society.

AMERICAN IMAGES OF THE NUER: RACE AND "REFUGEES"

It is a truism to state that within the host community, the Nuer have meant many different things to many different people. Just as the Nuer in Minnesota are a diverse group of individuals with a variety of goals, aspirations, and life experiences, so, too, it is impossible to stereotype American attitudes towards or interactions with the Nuer. With this caveat in mind, we can still explore some general factors that have shaped community attitudes toward the Nuer and inflected relations at a variety of levels. To Twin City residents the Nuer were a new and unfamiliar group, seen, at least initially, in terms of pre-existing notions. The Nuer were exotic, tribal Africans; they were refugees; they were black. These various ways, through which native Minnesotans were prepared to view the Nuer, colored relations in a number of complex ways.

That the Nuer are black, and that they are refugees stood out. It is true that Minnesota is a relatively progressive state socially and politically and does not have a history of significant problems with race relations. Nevertheless, as in any American community, racism certainly exists, even if it is less intense and less widespread than in many places. The Nuer mainly settled in the northern outer ring suburbs of the Twin Cities which are relatively homogeneously white. The sudden presence of a substantial number of black Africans was unnerving to many whose attitudes were shaped by their stereotypical views of African Americans. Indeed, I first learned that the Nuer had come to Minnesota through a Minnesota Public Radio report (8/25/95) on new immigrants that focused on the Nuer and issues of race. The report discussed the racist ways that some residents interpreted the behavior of the Nuer—including Nuer men's tendency to congregate in public spaces to discuss important matters—and the apprehension and misunderstandings that this created in the host community. In the radio report, an ESL instructor who worked closely with the Nuer noted:

> From the outside a group of black men is pretty scary to white residents, who think they're forming a gang or doing this for some illegal purposes . . . rather than saying this is how the community supports itself and this is how they communicate to each other on how to get your children immunized, and how to get your children in school, and how to get your car fixed.

Many Nuer men have an intimidating appearance, which probably fed into these stereotypes and racist attitudes. They are commonly well over six feet tall and, though not typically heavyset, frequently have a wiry, muscular build developed in the course of life in rural Africa. Various forms of scarification undertaken for both ritual and aesthetic reasons do not soften this look. In the course of male initiation, youths receive the distinctive scarring known as *gaar*, created by six cuts going ear to ear across their foreheads. Their faces are often decorated with hundreds of pinpoint scars known as *bir*, in some cases covering their entire faces with geometric patterns. Lower incisors are also typically removed, mainly for aesthetic purposes, giving their teeth a look that is unusual to most Americans. Thus, apart from the fact that they are black, many other factors make them stand out in a largely white community and reinforce stereotypes concerning both the dangerous nature of African Americans and the "savagery" of wild Africa.

Some racist incidents have occurred. I was shocked one day to arrive at the apartment of a Nuer friend and find the words "Die Nigger" scratched into the outside of his door. A Nuer middle school student complained of persistent harassment and intimidation that was motivated by, or at least inflected with, racism. Racism can also be an issue in the workplace. The Nuer employed in manual or industrial labor have complained of being "treated like animals," and that supervisors feel that blacks, and particularly newly arrived Africans, have no need for, or do not deserve, decent breaks on the job. A blatant incident occurred when Ganwar was injured after being thrown into a dumpster by white coworkers at an industrial job. His white supervisor chose to interpret this action as horseplay that had gotten out of hand, though Ganwar asserted that it had arisen out of tensions with fellow workers and that racism was one factor involved.

Racism is an underlying reality that the Nuer face, but it should not be overemphasized. Incidents have occurred, but they are few and far between. In fact, Africans are frequently viewed with substantially less racism by whites than African Americans. Negative stereotypes of African Americans often portray them as a dangerous,

Male initiation involves six deep cuts across the forehead from ear to ear leaving distinctive scars, *gaar*. Pinpoint scars, *bir*, are also made for aesthetic purposes.

criminal, ignorant underclass. In contrast, stereotypes of Africans are quite the opposite; they are often seen as simple, pious people who are particularly in need, and deserving of our assistance. On one hand, the "starving child" in Ethiopia or elsewhere epitomizes the obligation of wealthy nations to assist those in need. In contrast, inner-city African-American children as young as five years old have been characterized by some as a new generation of "super predators," as violent and amoral as the gang culture to which they are exposed in their neighborhoods (Canada 1998).

Due to these differences, the Nuer are more likely to meet with openness and acceptance among whites than African Americans. This does not mean, certainly, that racism is absent, but it is less intense and the stereotypes less divisive. While the strongest interpersonal relationships continue to be within the Nuer community, Nuer also develop friendships with both whites and African

Americans. When Nuer youths and unmarried men date Americans, which they do on occasion, they usually date white women. In many ways, the relationship of the Nuer to African Americans is more complex than their relationship to whites. On one hand, there is a tendency for younger Nuer to emulate the styles of African Americans, and when Nuer and African Americans are in contact in schools or elsewhere, there is frequently mutual interest in one another. On the other hand, the Nuer report instances of tension with some African Americans that far exceed those experienced with whites. Some Nuer families, who moved from the northern suburbs to the inner city in search of cheaper housing, have experienced almost daily harassment from African Americans.

In other states where Nuer populations are situated in inner-city environments, more tension, and sometimes violence, has resulted. For instance, some Nuer friends who moved to Omaha reported that they initially experienced harassment from members of the African-American community. They said this abated, however, when the Nuer bought guns, and made this fact known. The Nuer perceived that they were being taken for naïve, helpless newcomers, rather than as hardened survivors of a war-torn land. As one Nuer man described it, "We told them, 'We come from a violent country, so if you want [to fight] we are all right with that.'" The Nuer feel that they were able to earn respect in this way, and although little cooperation has developed between the Nuer and African-American community organizations in Omaha, by now there is also little violence.

Negative interactions between the Nuer and African Americans are often fed by stereotypes on both sides. African Americans have emphasized the "primitiveness" of the Nuer and accused them—since they had still been living in Africa—of being representatives of the people who had sold their ancestors into slavery. Some also expressed jealousy, assuming that the late model cars the Nuer struggle to buy were simply given to them as refugee assistance, while many native-born African Americans remain in poverty. By the same token, some Nuer have developed negative views of African Americans, a product, no doubt, of exposure to stereotypes in the wider culture. One Nuer man, for instance, explained to me how African Americans don't like to work but just want to collect welfare. Another recent African immigrant group to the Twin Cities, the Somalis, who have settled in the inner city in significant numbers, have had a tense and violent relationship with African Americans, based largely on these same kinds of conflicts.

That the Nuer are refugees also influences their reception by Minnesotans. Central to American and western popular conceptualizations of "the refugee" is that refugees are a special type of person, uniquely in need of aid, helpless victims of a maelstrom of international conflict far beyond their control. These images are broadly expressed in advertisements and other materials put out by organizations that provide services to refugees. Because these organizations are dependent on direct contributions and other forms of public support, it is in their interest to present an image of refugees that argues for their clear and unqualified need for aid. Most often, this involves focusing on refugees who Americans are most ready to perceive as victims, particularly women and children (Malkki 1995). While it is true that large portions of the world's refugee population are women and children, their representation in popular images of refugees is vastly disproportionate to their actual numbers. Among Sudanese refugees in the world today, for instance, the sex ratio is actually almost completely balanced (UNHCR 1998).

The actual nature of a refugee may, however, be very different from this popular image of a victim. A person does not successfully negotiate a war zone, live in harsh conditions in a refugee camp, and travel thousands of miles to seek permission to resettle in a new land by being passive and helpless. Rather, as we have seen, the Nuer have actively taken their fate into their own hands, and—despite the horrible conditions they have experienced—managed through their own strength and wits, to shape their lives in innovative and compelling ways.

In establishing relationships with members of the host community, the popularized refugee-as-victim image does not mesh with the flesh and blood refugee—an adept manipulator of his or her own destiny. An individual in the host community may wish to provide assistance to an imagined "refugee"—a person uniquely in need and deserving of aid—but the actual person encountered may be very different.

The experience of Earl, a white retiree, vividly illustrates this problem. Earl became involved with the Nuer in 1995, early in the resettlement process. When a call went out to local churches to assist with the resettlement of "Sudanese refugees," Earl responded to his pastor's request because he wanted to "do the work of the Lord." Earl had some interest in proselytism, as well, but more importantly felt that it was his Christian duty to assist those in need. He began to respond to calls from county social services to drive women and children to classes and child care and to deliver household items to families in need. Gradually his involvement deepened, but with it his frustration. Some of this stemmed from difficulties in communication and problems arranging logistics for people with a different sense of time than Earl's. More important, he increasingly felt that the Nuer were pressuring him to provide money or other gifts. In particular, he felt that a family with whom he had become especially close were trying to take advantage of him. He eventually became so frustrated that after more than two years of sincere and dedicated efforts to aid Nuer families, he stopped doing volunteer work entirely.

It is not difficult to understand Earl's frustration. He enjoyed his contact with the woman of the family and the children, but felt that the husband, in particular, was trying to take advantage of him. Especially after the family bought a car, he felt that he was being called on to do things for which the husband should have been responsible. This perception was accentuated when the husband was brought to court for domestic violence.

Cultural misunderstandings were also involved. Much of Earl's frustration stemmed from differences in the way that giving, receiving, and expressions of gratitude are constructed in Nuer and American culture. While there is a general belief in American culture that you should limit the scope and frequency of your requests—you shouldn't ask too often or for too much—in many traditional societies, including many African societies, no such etiquette exists. There, the dictum, "It doesn't hurt to ask," often rules the day. All that someone can do is say no. If you have something, there is some expectation that you will give, and if you need something, it is normal to ask. Members of these societies, and outsiders with extensive contact with them, learn to develop effective means for dealing with constant requests. During anthropological fieldwork in northern Kenya, for instance, I simply stopped carrying any coins or small bills with me unless I intended to give them away, or I had a very good explanation on hand as to why I could not give.

Seen in this context, behavior which might seem rude and manipulative to an American appears very different to the Nuer. Forced to survive in the difficult environment of refugee camps, one can only imagine how the ability to squeeze what one can out of one's social and physical world could be developed even further. The behavior which alienated Earl is all the more upsetting to Americans because it runs counter to understandings of what a refugee is. Seen as a passive victim in need of one's aid, Americans usually expect a refugee to be grateful, or at least not manipulative. This may be a reasonable expectation from the standpoint of American values, but is not in sync with the cultural background or life experiences of the Nuer.

FORMAL CONTEXTS OF INTERACTION

Social services has provided one of the most important venues for interaction between the Nuer and Americans. Since the Nuer have been heavily dependent on welfare, they have come into frequent contact with case workers, nurses, and social workers in their everyday life. The two social workers who were formally hired to work specifically with the Nuer, and the many informal volunteers, had in some senses a dual role. On one hand, they were seeking to help the Nuer to adapt to life in the United States—helping them to get household goods and to learn life skills appropriate to the United States and serving as a conduit for information on services available through various public and private programs. On the other hand, they were also cultural brokers, attempting to interpret and communicate the needs of the Nuer to Americans with whom the Nuer came into frequent contact.

Landlords are one of the most important groups with whom the task of building cultural bridges was crucial. The Nuer cannot help but come into contact with landlords, and the tenant–landlord relationship is often tense. In Sudan the Nuer build their own houses out of locally available materials, but in the United States they must depend on others for their housing needs. A few of the Nuer in Minnesota have been able to endure long waiting lists to get access to subsidized housing, but most rent apartments from private landlords.

Inherent difficulties are built into the landlord–tenant relationship. From the standpoint of landlords, the Nuer are far from ideal tenants. Particularly in the earliest days of resettlement, the Nuer were unfamiliar with how to care for carpets, walls, toilets, and the like. Landlords were concerned about damage to the apartment; they also became frustrated when the same problems developed again and again. After several repairs of a broken toilet, one landlord, for instance, found that a piece of a video game was lodged within it. The Nuer sometimes have large families which puts additional wear and tear on an apartment. Buol, for instance, at one point had over a dozen people living in his two-bedroom apartment for more than a month, when he was serving as a host for new arrivals from Africa.

Being black and foreign can also prejudice landlords against the Nuer—and cultural differences and difficulties in communication complicate matters. Because the housing market in the Twin Cities is tight, landlords can afford to be choosy in selecting tenants. One result is that the Nuer often find themselves in the worst available housing, particularly because their household budgets are so small. In the worst cases, the apartment is downright unhealthy. An apartment was rented to Peter Ruey after it had been flooded and not properly dried out, and subsequently a serious mold problem affected the health of his family. In fairness, landlords willing to rent to the Nuer have not always been "slumlords," desperate to find someone to fill their apartments. Some have been genuinely open to people from other cultures and prepared to be helpful and sympathetic to the Nuer in resolving problems arising from unfamiliar housing conditions.

Medical treatment is another area where the Nuer and Americans are by necessity brought into close contact. Health care has come in two principal forms for the Nuer in Minnesota. They visit clinics, mainly in the northern suburbs, and public health nurses make extensive home visits. While relations with public health workers have generally been good, health care in clinics has been more problematic.

Many of the conflicts in health care relate to cultural conflict and misunderstandings between health professionals and the Nuer. That health care can be a highly charged arena for intercultural conflict is vividly illustrated in *The Spirit Catches You and You Fall Down: The Story of a Hmong Girl, Her American Doctors and the Collision of Two Cultures* (Fadiman 1997). In this riveting drama, the fate of a young Hmong (southeast Asian) girl suffering from severe epilepsy hangs in the balance, caught up in the maelstrom of cultural conflict between her American doctors and her Hmong parents. Based in their Hmong culture, her parents understood the causes of illness and appropriate treatments in ways very different from the prescriptions of western medicine. Problems in communication and conflicts in styles of personal interaction complicated matters, and all the while the girl's condition deteriorated.

The types of issues which have arisen in Nuer health care are—so far—less dramatic than those faced by this Hmong family, but are still significant. Unlike the Hmong in Fadiman's account, the Nuer have generally been quite accepting of whatever treatment is recommended to them, perhaps even more than Americans. Language barriers, however, have been a severe problem, especially in the earliest stage of resettlement when no interpreters were available. Even when Nuer men conversant in English were hired as interpreters, problems persisted. The interpreters were not professionally trained; sporadic work schedules made them difficult to retain; and the gender of the interpreter was an impediment to the openness of female patients until a female Nuer English speaker was identified and induced to move to Minnesota from another state.

In the suburban hospitals that the Nuer use, practitioners have usually had little contact with immigrants. Many doctors and nurses have little patience in dealing with people who speak English poorly and are unfamiliar with American medical care. "Who ARE these people, and WHY ARE they here? If they can't speak English, WHY ARE they here?" was the comment of one nurse/receptionist at a north suburban clinic. Although more overt than most, she expressed the general attitude that the Nuer have experienced from many health professionals. The Nuer have frequently been ignored at clinics. In one case, a man who had only recently come to Minnesota was stranded at a clinic when his taxi (which was provided by Medical Assistance) did not show up. Rather than try to help him get another one, the staff chose, instead, to ignore his problem and just let the cleaning crew close up around him. Fortunately, a public health nurse who had come to check on him was able to take him home.

The unequal power relations between provider and patient can make health care a particularly difficult environment for the Nuer. The culture of health care places high expectations on patients. For instance, they must follow directions closely and unwaveringly, finishing medicine even after they feel well. In Africa, patients simply come to clinics when they are open and are treated on a "first come, first served" basis. In the United States you must make an appointment and arrive on time. As was discussed in Chapter 3, Nuer notions about time are quite different from typical American ones. It is an understatement to say that (as in many African cultures) punctuality is not highly valued in a Nuer village setting. In the United States this often translates into missed appointments or missed taxis to take them to their appointments. At the same time, the expectation of punctuality is not typically met by the health care providers themselves (as anyone who has ever arrived on time, only to wait 30 to 45 minutes in a doctor's waiting room, can attest). The Nuer often think that having a 3:00 appointment means that (assuming they are there at 3:00) they will see a medical professional at 3:00. When they are left waiting, the Nuer often feel that they are being treated in a disrespectful way. The recent domination of American health care by HMOs has added to problems in the health care environment because their emphasis on providing quick, efficient, uniform service is out of sync with a population, like the Nuer, having a variety of special needs.

Not surprisingly, interactions in hospitals and clinics are often characterized by high levels of tension. There have been many instances of outright rude behavior toward Nuer patients by medical personnel who did not have the time, patience, or respect to treat the Nuer in the same manner afforded to American patients. This has not, of course, been uniformly true—and the Nuer tend to maintain a high level of respect for doctors—but discourteous treatment has, unfortunately, frequently characterized Nuer experiences in American clinics.

Home health care provided by public health nurses has, happily, been less of a problem. The counties in which the Nuer live have recruited nurses having a particular interest in diverse communities to work with the Nuer. They make frequent visits to Nuer homes to check on their health (particularly those on public assistance) and provide information on such things as diet and child health. Generally, these women have enjoyed very good relationships with the Nuer, who have appreciated the nurses' personal commitment and openness, as well as the services they have provided.

Nonetheless, misunderstandings and tensions can occasionally arise. This is illustrated by an experience of Linnea, a public health nurse who was among the first to work with the Nuer. After finishing up a late Friday afternoon visit to a Nuer family, they suggested that she go upstairs to meet a newly arrived family who had just moved into their building to see if they had any immediate problems. Linnea was reluctant, since by then it was 6:00, and she was eager to wrap things up and go home for the weekend. But she agreed to go upstairs, where she met the family and encountered their terribly sick infant. The baby had a high fever, and Linnea feared that without treatment the baby would not live. She immediately flew into emergency mode, dialed 911 and—to the surprise and dismay of the family—an ambulance arrived, and their child was whisked away. The Nuer family was, to say the least, not happy about this course of events, or with Linnea's role in it. From their standpoint it was presumptuous for her to take authority away from the child's own parents in that way. The child, however, was treated for a parasitic infection and recovered.

Relations were smoothed between Linnea and the child's parents, who were able to see the value of what she had done, even if it was in some ways in contradiction to Nuer values and personal styles.

NUER REFUGEES IN AMERICAN CHURCHES

Religion is a salient, shared symbol, bridging the gap between Nuer and Americans. When Dak Lut refused the help of his well-meaning neighbor in his first days in the United States (described in Chapter 2) it was the Bible that served as a potent symbol of virtue and good intent in ameliorating Dak's fears.

The church provides perhaps the only continuity between Nuer life in Africa and Minnesota. While the context of church, the activities that go on there, and the nature of membership are very different, there is a commonality of worship in Minnesota and Africa not found in other areas of Nuer life. Celebrations at Christmas or Easter are among the few events which bring most of the Nuer in Minnesota together at one time—and these events occur in churches. Moreover, church represents one of the few things that Nuer and Americans have in common. Indeed, it is essentially the only arena of intense interaction between the Nuer and Americans which is voluntary in nature. The Nuer have little choice in entering into interaction with Americans at work, at social service agencies, and school. At the same time, Americans in these contexts are doing a job. This is not the case in church. While relationships between the Nuer and Americans in church contexts are certainly complex, they come closest to genuine cross-cultural friendship and camaraderie than any other area of life.

Most Nuer in Minnesota are Christians, or at least nominally so. Generally, they grew up following the traditional Nuer religion and later converted in the context of contact with missionaries or their African catechists. Frequently this occurred in schools in Sudan or in camps in Ethiopia. Traditional Nuer religion centers on a deity referred to as Kuoth. Kuoth is not so much a personified being as a form of ubiquitous Spirit, found throughout nature—in the sky, in the rain, and in the wind (Johnson 1994; Evans-Pritchard 1956). Kuoth is also manifested in a variety of lesser spirits that are believed to have fallen from the sky. Foremost among these is Deng, who is often believed to occupy individual prophets.

Missionization of the Nuer began in the colonial period, but with few real successes until the 1960s. Christian proselytism occurred only at three mission schools, which enjoyed little popularity. Ironically, the successful spread of Christianity among the Nuer accompanied government actions aimed at just the opposite. When the northern, Islamic military government expelled foreign missionaries in 1963 to 1964, the few southern Sudanese who had become Christians took the lead in running churches. They were able to bring Christianity to rural areas in ways which were much more familiar to the Nuer than the approach which European and American missionaries had used. Christian beliefs in many ways became fused with the traditional theology of Nuer religion, while Christian leaders began to assume some of the functions previously held by traditional prophets (Johnson 1994).

Most of the Nuer in Minnesota call themselves Christians and attend a Christian worship service on a regular basis. Only one man I met claimed to have no involvement in Christianity. When asked his religious affiliation for a survey, he responded, "If you have to put down something, put that I follow Ngundeng," a great Nuer religious leader of the late nineteenth century who was renowned for his spiritual powers, gift of prophecy, and political leadership (Johnson 1994). Prophets such as Ngundeng and his son, Gwek (who was killed by Arab agents of the British colonizers of Sudan) are greatly respected by the Nuer in Minnesota, regardless of the importance of Christianity in their lives. When I first made contact with the Nuer in late 1995, many were excited to learn of a book that I owned, *Nuer Prophets* (Johnson 1994), which recounts the history of Ngundeng, Gwek, and other prophets. Among my first identities in the community was "the guy with the Ngundeng book." The Nuer in Sudan often see parallels in the teachings of their prophets and the teaching of Jesus. Even though there are contradictions between Christianity and indigenous Nuer beliefs—such as beliefs in animal sacrifice in Nuer religion—both may be embraced by the same individual.

The Nuer belong to a wide range of Christian denominations. Most prominent are Presbyterians, Evangelicals, and Seventh Day Adventists. Presbyterians have the oldest and most established missions in southern Sudan, having started their work in the 1930s. In Minnesota, the Nuer also attend other churches which do not have traditionally strong ties to southern Sudan.

The depth of involvement in the Christian faith and knowledge of Christian theology differ widely among the Nuer. The Old and New Testament have been translated into Nuer, and there are many Nuer hymns, as well. Calling oneself a Christian can be very important to self-identification, and may lead to important changes in one's lifestyle. Seventh Day Adventists, for instance, emphasize abstinence from alcohol, despite the importance of its use in Nuer life. Church also provides an important context for gathering regularly, and for celebrating holidays and special occasions.

How and why particular Nuer are involved in church, as well as why they choose the churches they attend, are complex matters which go beyond simple matters of faith. Beyond long-standing religious affiliation derived from the particular form of Christianity dominant in their Sudanese village, the Nuer often received forms of assistance from other churches in the process of being a refugee. In the United States, as well, material and spiritual interests may become interwoven in the context of church.

Churches were often involved with the Nuer in the very process of resettlement. In many cases, congregations as a whole, or individual members within them, took responsibility for sponsoring a refugee, which was instrumental in a refugee gaining permission to resettle. Sponsors also provided assistance in the very earliest stages of resettlement. Frequently, then, a tie was forged to a particular congregation even before a Nuer had ever stepped foot in the United States. Because a church sponsored an individual, however, did not mean he or she inevitably joined it on arrival in Minnesota. The Nuer tended to seek out congregations of the denomination to which they had been exposed in Sudan, most commonly Presbyterian. Frequently these were the same denominations which may have sponsored them, but not necessarily so.

Whatever the process of joining a congregation, integrating within them could be difficult, with language and cultural differences presenting often impenetrable barriers. This is illustrated by experiences within one congregation in a northern Twin Cities suburb. Understandably, the Nuer wished to have their own service, which they would perform themselves in the Nuer language. The church gave them a space where they could worship, and the Nuer began a regular Sunday service in Nuer. Unfortunately, conflict quickly arose. Unlike the service of the all-white congregation, the Nuer service was a raucous, lively affair, with spirited singing to the pounding beat of African drums. This proved incompatible with the English service going on upstairs, and the minister was upset to have the tranquility of the chapel interrupted by persistent drumming—not to mention the effect this had on his sermon. The Nuer did not fully understand the nature of the problem, and felt that they were being treated like second-class citizens by being asked to worship at a different time than the rest of the church. Bad feelings arose, and the Nuer decided to move to a different church of the same denomination. Unfortunately, the same problem arose again, and bad feelings once again ensued. Only with the intervention of an experienced university-educated Nuer mediator from another state was it made clear that, since they were receiving a space to worship free of charge, they should honor the request to change the time of the Nuer service.

The numbers attending this service dwindled, however, and eventually the Nuer service at the church stopped altogether. Partially, this was due to outmigration to Nebraska, which substantially reduced the number of potential congregants. Many, however, moved on to a different church. This new church, surprisingly, was so eager to get Nuer members that its leaders bent over backwards to accommodate the Nuer on the desired time for their service—even going so far as to change the time of the English service so that there would not be a conflict.

Economic factors can also be important in attracting congregants. Churches have come to be seen as an avenue for gaining access to various kinds of resources, a view which goes back to the earliest stages of resettlement. In many cases, church sponsors provided the initial household goods that the Nuer needed to set up a home in the United States. Many churches continued to collect and distribute goods to the Nuer well after initial resettlement and were often willing to provide emergency aid in order to repair automobiles needed for employment, or to make rent payments to avoid eviction. For churches wishing to attract Nuer members, the effectiveness of material incentives was also clear.

In the case of the church that lost its Nuer members, the final blow centered on the issue of a van. As Nuer membership dwindled, a handful of young men tried to revitalize the congregation and return other Nuer to the church. In order to do this, they argued, they needed a van. With the van they could provide transportation so that families would be able to attend the Sunday service more easily. These young men wished to use the van during the week for other purposes as well. There was some willingness on the part of the congregation to provide a van, but several factors made it impossible. While the church still had some money from a denominational grant for assisting Nuer resettlement, there was not enough left for a van. Church leaders hoped that they might get more money from the denomination but this didn't work. The Nuer congregation was simply not viable, the denomination leadership argued, citing the attrition and low levels of financial commitment from the Nuer themselves. The young men finally left the church and moved to a new congregation where, promptly, they received a van.

What is clear is that spiritual relationships have become deeply entangled in the negotiation of material ones. Material inducements have sometimes been used to draw Nuer members to churches, though even these should not be seen as crassly instrumental. A Christian philosophy that you cannot reach someone's soul if their stomach is empty has informed the efforts of many in serving the Nuer; if the means are sometimes material, the end is a higher one. And while economic interests are involved in the tendency of some Nuer to shift their religious affiliation, in general the Nuer desire to participate in church life is driven by a deep emphasis on spirituality.

Churches, for their part, may find opportunities in becoming involved with the Nuer. The Nuer can provide international links, as well as the opportunity to pursue humanitarian and proselytizing goals outside of the United States. To some denominations, Sudan represents a wonderful chance both to do humanitarian work and to spread the gospel, and the Nuer in Minnesota are ready allies of missionary work. Several official delegations from Minnesota churches have traveled to camps in Ethiopia and Kenya, as well as to Sudan itself, in order to find out about ways their congregations might help the Nuer living there and perhaps establish their churches in Africa. The Nuer in Minnesota have helped organize these efforts, and on one occasion accompanied church officials on their mission.

TRANSFORMING AMERICANS

If the lives of the Nuer have been transformed in Minnesota, so, too, have Minnesotans who worked with them been changed in the process. "They have given me much more than I have ever given them," is a frequent statement of Minnesotans who have worked with the Nuer—a sentiment that, if cliche, speaks to the significance of this involvement in their lives. The Nuer have provided them with the opportunity to learn about another culture, as well as a chance to get to know people whose company they enjoyed and who they admired for perseverance and strength in their lives as refugees. At the same time, it has been very meaningful humanitarian work to many Americans involved with the Nuer. While most Americans who have worked with the Nuer have done so as part of their jobs (even if they chose that particular assignment), others have undertaken it simply as volunteer work which they found personally important—for instance, Elspeth, an elderly woman who organized her own ESL classes in Nuer homes and made frequent visits to provide many other forms of assistance.

One of the most interesting cases of an American who was transformed through work with the Nuer is Kelly, an American woman in her thirties. Though she had little international background, through work with the Nuer at her church she became drawn into a network of relations extending to Sudan itself. She became interested in the Nuer and increasingly involved in work with them when they started to attend her church. Through these contacts she became interested in the situation in Sudan itself and actually made contact with the leader of one of the major rebel factions in Sudan through a Nuer man in Minnesota. About a year after she started working with the Nuer, she decided to travel to Sudan on a fact-finding mission. Amazingly, she was able to meet both with rebel leaders and high officials in the Sudanese government, as well as to travel to war-torn regions and visit Nuer in the squatter settlements of Khartoum. Bob, a young American man, also saw his life transformed by work with the Nuer. He started volunteer work soon after the Nuer arrived and quickly made many close friends. Indeed, he ended up becoming a roommate of several young Nuer men and left Minneapolis with them when they decided to move to another city.

The impact of the Nuer on the lives of Americans was evident in the spring of 1997 when nearly half of the Nuer community abruptly emigrated to Nebraska—primarily because of opportunities for subsidized housing. There was no question that many Americans who worked with the Nuer felt a deep loss after this development. The loss of particular friends was, in many ways, less important to them than the extent to which they were forced to question the meaning of the work they had been doing. Was their help unneeded? Had they not helped enough? Could other people or other states better provide for the needs of the Nuer? Several predicted that after a short time the Nuer would realize that things were better in Minnesota and return. Bea, a woman from the church whose Nuer congregation stopped attending, expressed profound disappointment and sadness about her work with the Nuer. Her disappointment centered on what she saw as the failure of her church's work with the Nuer—that the Nuer could not find what they needed in her denomination and, so, went elsewhere, where others served their needs.

CONCLUSION

Stereotypes often portray the relationship between immigrants and the host community as one of inherent conflict—that as newcomers arrive they disrupt the lives of long-time residents and tension is inevitable. The experience of the Nuer has shown this to be far from the case. Relations between immigrants and established residents are highly dependent on the contexts of interaction with the host community and on the mediating institutions that structure relations between immigrants and hosts (Lamphere 1992). While some interactions between the Nuer and Americans have been characterized by significant, albeit usually muted, tension—for instance, landlord–tenant relationships—the predominant experience has been quite the opposite. Rather than being regarded as a threat to the community, the Nuer usually have been seen as a group requiring special attention and special charity.

The arrival of the Nuer in a place like Minnesota is as strange for Minnesotans as it is for the Nuer. In the largely white, Nordic, middle-class suburbs, the Americans whom the Nuer have encountered have struggled to make sense of the Nuer's arrival, often drawing on pre-existing stereotypes, images of Africa, and conceptualizations of "the refugee." The fact that these have come together to produce predominantly positive encounters with Americans can be attributed to a variety of factors. Certainly the fact that the Nuer community remained small, colored perceptions of the Nuer. Indeed, in the earliest stages of resettlement— when the magnitude of Nuer immigration was unclear, and when the presence of only a few blacks was a warning sign to some established residents—trepidation did characterize the attitudes of some towards the Nuer. Had the Nuer community continued its rapid growth, there may have been more frequent and intense friction. As it was, contact was limited mainly to interactions that were largely voluntary in nature. Consequently, the Nuer came to be seen in the eyes of those Americans with whom they had contact as more of an opportunity—to learn about another culture and to do good—than as an imposition on their community.

7

Looking Forward

"If there is peace, then I will go back," says Ganwar, expressing the sentiments of many Nuer in Minnesota. For most Nuer, there are things which they value about life in the United States—the opportunity for education, to work, to have an apartment and a car. Most importantly, the United States is a place of peace, a sanctuary from the bitter fighting that has plagued their country since before they were born. Whatever advantages they enjoy in the United States, however, for many their goal remains to return to their homes and to a more familiar way of life. Nyabuom Diew echoes the sentiment of Ganwar and many others in declaring "I will go back if things get better." The difficulties of raising children in the United States, the constant need to work, and the expense of rent and other necessities make a return to Sudan an enticing dream for many, along with the prospect of being reunited with those they left behind. Others, who have been able to take advantage of their time in the United States to earn a college degree, see a peaceful Sudan as a place where higher education will be a more precious commodity that will be more valuable there than in the United States. As one noted "If you work in a meat packing plant but you have a degree, you think you should go back and get a government job." News from Sudan, and in particular the progress of peace talks to end the civil war, are watched closely—if skeptically—in the hopes that the results will bring the opportunity to return to a peaceful and productive life in southern Sudan. While the 2005 Comprehensive Peace Agreement—ending the war on paper, if not yet bringing security on the ground—is now a source of considerable optimism, skepticism still remains as to whether it will bring true peace.

For some, however, the advantages of the American lifestyle outweigh any desire to return to friends, family, and a rural African lifestyle, at least on a permanent basis. This is particularly true of younger men who have been successful in finding good jobs and who wish to raise their children with easy access to educational opportunities. Dak Lut, for instance, one of the earliest arrivals in the United States, is already preparing to take his citizenship examination. Chuol Mut hopes to meet an American woman whom he might marry, with the idea that the skills and independence of a native-born wife will make her a more suitable partner for his planned life in the United States. James Tap awaits the end of the war, at which time he plans to visit his home area, but he is firmly committed to permanently settling into a life in the United States.

Not all young men, of course, are so optimistic about their new life. I am reminded of Peter, a young man in his early twenties, whom I interviewed in the dim light of a cold, late November day in his studio apartment in a public housing complex in Minneapolis. He had studied in a secondary school in Ethiopia and came to the United States prepared to seize the opportunities it presented. While living in another state where he was working in a slaughterhouse, he became clinically depressed and moved to Minnesota partially because of treatment opportunities available there. Asked about the differences he saw between life in Africa and life in the United States, Peter sat on his bed, staring straight ahead into the darkness, "I only know that in Africa I was always happy, and now I am always sad."

There are many challenges that the Nuer have faced, in their home areas ravaged by war, in the refugee camps to which they fled to safety, and in the long and difficult journey that brought them to peace. In resettling in a cold and strange land, they have faced and continue to face additional challenges—from learning how to use an American kitchen, to gaining economic independence in a country so different from Sudan. They have had to learn how to negotiate a culture as centered on the automobile as their own culture is on cows. And they have had to deal with the psychological trauma of war and resettlement in an alien culture while trying to forge new forms of community from the remnants shattered in a decade of flight, reshaping family relationships in a very different social, cultural, and legal milieu.

There have been successes as well as failures at both the individual and community level. Some Nuer families have been able to attain economic self-sufficiency, even to the point of purchasing a home. Achieving economic self-sufficiency while working long hours at generally low-paying, unattractive jobs has required hard work, tremendous discipline, and perhaps some degree of good fortune. Many others, however, continue to struggle to make ends meet—still totally dependent on public assistance, unable to maintain steady employment, and plagued by bad luck and personal difficulties. While some families have adjusted relatively comfortably to new roles for men and women, greater equality between the sexes, and a home life in which domestic violence is not tolerated, others have found this transition to be more difficult. In all of these areas, transformations are ongoing as the Nuer make their own futures while waiting to see what the future holds.

References

Anoka County Human Services Center (ACHSC)
n.d.   Calculation Worksheet, MFIP Statewide Grant. Blaine, MN.

Beidelman, T. O.
1966   The Ox and Nuer Sacrifice. *Man* 1:453–467.
1971   Nuer Priests and Prophets: Charisma, Authority and Power Among the Nuer. In T. O. Beidelman (ed.), *The Translation of Culture* (pp. 375–415). London: Tavistock.

Benson, Janet
1994   Reinterpreting Gender: Southeast Asian Refugees and American Society. In Linda Camino and Ruth Krulfeld (eds.), *Reconstructing Lives, Recapturing Meanings: Refugee Identity, Gender and Culture Change* (pp. 75–96). Basel, Switzerland: Gordon and Breach.

Burr, J. M. and R. O. Collins
1995   *Requiem for Sudan: War, Drought and Disaster Relief on the Nile*. Boulder, Co: Westview Press.

Canada, Geoffrey
1998   *Reaching Up for Manhood: Transforming the Lives of Boys in America*. Boston: Beacon Press.

Collier, Jane
1988   *Marriage and Inequality in Classless Societies*. Palo Alto: Stanford University Press.

Cuno, Kenneth
1997   *Refugees*. In Charles Stewart and Peter Fritzsche (eds.), *Imagining the Twentieth Century*. Urbana, IL: University of Illinois Press.

Daly, M. W. and Ahmad Alawad Sikainga, eds.
1993   *Civil War in Sudan*. London: British Academic Press.

Deng, Francis Mading
1995   *War of Visions: Conflict of Identity in Sudan.* Washington, D.C.: Brookings Institute.

di Leonardo, Micaela
1979   Methodology and Misinterpretation of Women's Status: A Case Study of Goodenough and the Definition of Marriage. *American Ethnologist* 6(4):627–637.
1991   Introduction: Gender, Culture and Political Economy: Feminist Anthropology in Historical Perspective. In Micaela di Leonardo (ed.), *Gender at the Crossroads of Knowledge: Feminist Anthropology in the Postmodern Era.* Berkeley and Los Angeles: University of California Press.
2000   *Exotics at Home: Anthropologies, Others and American Modernity.* Chicago: University of Chicago Press.

Duany, Wal
1992   Neither Palaces Nor Prisons: The Constitution of Order Among the Nuer. Ph.D. Dissertation, Indiana University.

Evans Pritchard, E. E.
1940   *The Nuer.* Oxford: Oxford University Press.
1951   *Kinship and Marriage Among the Nuer.* Oxford: Oxford University Press.
1956   *Nuer Religion.* Oxford: Clarendon Press.

Fadiman, Anne
1997   *The Spirit Catches You and You Fall Down.* New York: Farrar, Strauss and Giroux.

Farnham, Dana
n.d.   *Who Represents the Sudanese?* Unpublished m.s., San Diego, California.

Gordon, Peter, Harry Richardson and Gang Yu
1998   Metropolitan and Non-metropolitan Employment Trends in the U.S.: Recent Evidence and Implications. *Urban Studies* 35(7):1037–1058.

Gough, K.
1971   Nuer Kinship: A Re-examination. In T. O. Beidelman (ed.), *The Translation of Culture* (pp. 79–121). London: Tavistock.

Gupta, Akhil and James Ferguson (eds.)
1997   *Anthropological Locations: Boundaries and Grounds of a Field Science.* Berkeley: University of California Press.

Haines, David W.
1982   Southeast Asian Refugees in the United States: The Interaction of Kinship and Public Policy. *Anthropological Quarterly* 55(3):170–181.

1985   Towards Integration into American Society. In David
        Haines (ed.), *Refugees in the United States: A Reference
        Handbook* (pp. 37–55). Westport, CT: Greenwood Press.

Harris, Chauncy
1997   "The Nature of Cities" and Urban Geography in the Last
        Half Century. *Urban Geography 18*(1):15–35.

Highway Loss Data Institute (HLDI)
1993   Insurance Collision Report R93–2. Arlington, VA:
        Highway Loss Data Institute.

Hutchinson, Sharon
1990   Rising Divorce Among the Nuer, 1936–1983. *Man*
        25:393–411.
1992   War Through the Eyes of the Dispossessed: Three
        Stories of Survival. *Disasters 15*:166–171.
1996   *Nuer Dilemmas: Coping with War, Money and the State.*
        Berkeley: University of California Press.

Immigration and Naturalization Service (INS)
1997   Statistical Yearbook 1996. Washington, DC: INS.

James, Wendy
1997   The Names of Fear: Memory, History and the
        Ethnography of Feeling Among Uduk Refugees. *Journal
        of the Royal Anthropological Institute 3*(1).

Johnson, Douglas
1994   *Nuer Prophets.* Oxford: Oxford University Press.

Karp, Ivan and K. Maynard
1983   Reading *The Nuer. Current Anthropology* 24:481–503.

Kelly, Raymond
1985   *The Nuer Conquest.* Ann Arbor: University of Michigan
        Press.

Kok, Peter Nyot
1992   Adding Fuel to the Conflict: Oil, War and Peace in Sudan.
        In M. Doornbos, L. Cliffe, Abdel Gaffer M. Ahmed and
        J. Markakis (eds.), *Beyond Conflict in the Horn* (pp. 104–112).
        The Hague: Institute of Social Studies.

Koltyk, Jo Ann
1998   *New Pioneers in the Heartland: Hmong Life in Wisconsin.*
        Needham Heights, MA: Allyn and Bacon.

Lamphere, Louise
1992   Introduction: The Shaping of Diversity. in Louise
        Lamphere (ed.) *Structuring Diversity* (pp. 1–34). Chicago:
        University of Chicago Press.

Malkki, Liisa
1995   *Purity and Exile: Violence, Memory and National Cosmology Among Hutu Refugees in Tanzania.* Chicago: University of Chicago Press.

Mayer, Phillip
1971   *Townsmen or Tribesman.* Oxford: Oxford University Press.

Mead, Margaret
1928   *Coming of Age in Samoa.* New York: William Morrow.

Metcalf, Peter
2001   Global "Disjunctive" and the "Sites" of Anthropology. *Cultural Anthropology* 16(2):165–182.

Miller, Daniel
1998   Coca Cola: A Black Sweet Drink from Trinidad. In Daniel Miller (ed.) *Material Cultures: Why Some Things Matter* (pp. 169–188). Chicago: University of Chicago Press.

Min, Pyong Gap
1998   *Changes and Conflicts: Korean Immigrant Families in New York.* Needham Heights, MA: Allyn and Bacon.

Newcomer, P. J.
1972   The Nuer Are Dinka: An Esssay on Origins and Environmental Determinism. *Man* 7:5–11.

Preston, Valerie, S. McLafferty and X. F. Liu
1998   Geographical Barriers to Employment for American-born and Immigrant Workers. *Urban Studies* 35(3)529–545.

Reiter, Rayna Rapp, ed.
1975   *Toward an Anthropology of Women.* New York: Monthly Review Press.

Rosaldo, Michele and Louise Lamphere, eds.
1974   *Women, Culture and Society.* Palo Alto: Stanford University Press.

Sahlins, Marshall
1961   The Segmentary Lineage: An Organization of Predatory Expansion. *American Anthropologist* 63:322–345.

Southall, Ian
1986   The Illusion of Nath Agnation. *Ethnology* 25:1–20.

Stoller, Paul
1997   *Sensuous Scholarship.* Philadelphia: University of Pennsylvania Press.

Strathern, Marilyn
1988   *The Gender of the Gift: Problems of Gender and Problems of Society in Melanesia.* Berkeley and Los Angeles: University of California Press.

Swedenburg, Ted and Smadar Lavie (eds.)
1996   *Displacement, Diaspora* and *Geographies of Identity*. Durham, NC: Duke University Press.

Thomas, Ralph
n.d.   *Automobile Repossession: A Guide for Professionals*. Internet published book at http://www.pimall.com/nais/n.repo.html.

United Nations High Commission for Refugees (UNHCR)
1998   Refugees and Others of Concern to the UNHCR: Statistical Overview 1997. Geneva: UNHCR.
2006   Return and Reintegration of Sudanese Refugees and IDP's to Southern Sudan and Protection of IDP's in Khartoum and Kassala States of Sudan. United Nations: Geneva, Switzerland.

United States Committee for Refugees (USCR)
1998   Country Reports: Sudan. Washington, DC: USCR.
2006   *World Refugee Survey 2005*. U.S. Commission for Refugees: Washington, D.C.